PENGUIN

LOVE VISIONS

ADVISORY EDITOR: BETTY RADICE

GEOFFREY CHAUCER was born in London, the son of a vintner, in about 1342. He is known to have been a page to the Countess of Ulster in 1357, and Edward III valued him highly enough to pay a part of his ransom in 1360, after he had been captured fighting in France.

It was probably in France that Chaucer's interest in poetry was aroused. Certainly he soon began to translate the long allegorical poem of courtly love, the *Roman de la Rose*. His literary experience was further increased by visits to the Italy of Boccaccio on the King's business, and he was well-read in several languages and on many topics, such as astronomy, medicine, physics and alchemy.

Chaucer rose in royal employment, and became a knight of the shire for Kent (1385–6) and a Justice of the Peace. A lapse of favour during the temporary absence of his steady patron, John of Gaunt (to whom he was connected by his marriage), gave him time to begin organizing his unfinished *Canterbury Tales*. Later his fortunes revived, and at his death in 1400 he was buried in Westminster Abbey.

The order of his works is uncertain, but they include *The Book of the Duchess*, *The House of Fame*, *The Parliament of Fowls*, *Troilus and Criseyde* and a translation of Boethius's *De Consolatione Philosophiae*.

BRIAN STONE wrote his first book, *Prisoner from Alamein*, which had a foreword by Desmond MacCarthy, in 1944. After the war, during which he was decorated, he entered the teaching profession and taught English in boys' schools for eleven years. He then trained teachers for ten years at Loughborough and Brighton. In 1969 he became a founder member of the Open University, where he was Reader of Literature for the rest of his professional life. Besides Penguin Critical Studies of Chaucer and Keats, he has four other verse translations to his credit in the Penguin Classics: modern English renderings of *Sir Gawain and the Green Knight*; *Medieval English*

Verse; *The Owl and the Nightingale, Cleanness, St Erkenwald*; and *King Arthur's Death: Alliterative 'Morte Arthure' and Stanzaic 'Le Morte Arthur'*.

Brian Stone died in London in March 1995. In its obituary the *Independent* described him as 'a brilliant teacher, an enthusiast for good English and an exceptionally brave man. He was unmistakable with his jaunty, determined, one-legged walk and air of buoyant optimism.'

GEOFFREY CHAUCER

Love Visions

THE BOOK OF THE DUCHESS
THE HOUSE OF FAME
THE PARLIAMENT OF BIRDS
THE LEGEND OF GOOD WOMEN

Translated with an Introduction and Notes by
BRIAN STONE

PENGUIN BOOKS

PENGUIN BOOKS

Published by the Penguin Group
Penguin Books Ltd, 27 Wrights Lane, London W8 5TZ, England
Penguin Putnam Inc., 375 Hudson Street, New York, New York 10014, USA
Penguin Books Australia Ltd, Ringwood, Victoria, Australia
Penguin Books Canada Ltd, 10 Alcorn Avenue, Toronto, Ontario, Canada M4V 3B2
Penguin Books (NZ) Ltd, 182–190 Wairau Road, Auckland 10, New Zealand

Penguin Books Ltd, Registered Offices: Harmondsworth, Middlesex, England

This translation first published 1983
9 10 8

Translation and editorial matter copyright © Brian Stone, 1983
All rights reserved

Printed in England by Clays Ltd, St Ives plc
Filmset in Monophoto Photina

CONTENTS

FOREWORD

In offering translations of Chaucer's four 'love visions', I should like at the outset to make the fullest possible acknowledgement to the late F. N. Robinson for his great edition of *The Poetical Works of Chaucer* (Houghton Mifflin Co., Boston, 1933; second edition 1954). I have always returned to it after consulting other editions; when I have quoted him here, the page numbers refer to the first edition. As was almost inevitable, at times I have drawn on his work indirectly, without specific reference, and I trust that this grateful acknowledgement to his extraordinarily full and informative scholarship will compensate for any formal omission of mine. My debt to other scholars is, I hope, made clear whenever I quote them, and the value I attach to their work is signalled by naming them in my select bibliography.

Of recent years, interest in work of Chaucer's other than *The Canterbury Tales* has increased. Several translations of *Troilus and Criseyde* have appeared, and both that great poem and the early love visions are now occasionally set texts, not only in universities and colleges, but in schools. General public interest in our medieval heritage seems to increase year by year. So there is every justification for translating the love visions.

I have kept support material to the minimum, and I hope that the Notes will further understanding and enjoyment of the poems. In discussing classical references I have tried to give generally accepted versions rather than to be exhaustive concerning alternatives, or to define specifically medieval meanings – unless the latter are crucial to the poetic reference.

A word on the problem of verse translation, which Chaucer himself faced whenever he borrowed and adapted a well-known passage from Ovid, or Froissart, or Jean de Meun, or Dante, or Boccaccio. Chaucer's iambics, whether in four- or five-foot lines, run with an accentual freedom which his French peers eschewed or lacked, and for which he thought fit to apologize. Chaucer was responding to the nature of modern English, which was then in the making, and was breaking out of moulds set by Norman French conquerors and native, slightly archaic, exemplars. So in re-rendering Chaucer in twentieth-century English I too claim my freedoms, though always, I hope, in the interest of representing him as accurately as possible. To be precise: I have generally written iambics, and kept the right number of feet in the line; I have always looked for perfect rhyme, but have allowed imperfection when that seemed the only way of keeping decently close to original meaning; in including Chaucer's catalogues of proper names, I have abandoned rhyme almost completely when forced to by the fact that the form and pronunciation of the names have changed since his time. The great difficulty when translating such a shape-shifter as Chaucer, whose tone can change from lofty pathos to farce almost from one line to the next, is to hit the centre of poetic feeling with the appropriate vocabulary of today (with the occasional archaism, to be frank). The attempt leads into advanced interpretation as well as poetic invention, and in both matters I must submit to judgement.

The Open University   Brian Stone
April 1982

INTRODUCTION

We know more about Chaucer's life than Shakespeare's.
Shadow and surmise, so often met by inquirers into the circum-
stances in which our first poet lived and worked, loom lightlier
over the life of our earlier great poet. Chaucer, who was born in
the early 1340s and died in 1400, spent his life in and around
London and the Court, employed as esquire when young, and
later as soldier, diplomat and civil servant, by such people as
Prince Lionel, Edward III, Richard II and especially John of
Gaunt – men whose first language was French, which was
therefore the language of their courts, a circumstance which
enhances Chaucer's achievement. In the last year of his life,
Chaucer served Henry IV. He travelled in the royal service to
France and Italy, and probably met most of the English, French
and Italian poetic master spirits of the age. He knew Gower,
Strode, Froissart and Deschamps, probably met De Granson and
Machaut, and may well have met Boccaccio and Petrarch. In
view of the evidence that he led a busy life in the precincts of
power for thirty years or so, his poetic output is surprisingly
large – the equivalent of about twelve Shakespeare plays.

The four long poems here presented in translation span nearly
the whole of Chaucer's working life, 'The Book of the Duchess'
dating from 1369–70, and the revised Prologue to 'The Legend
of Good Women' from 1393–4. But the latter, since the
Legends themselves are generally agreed to have been written
earlier, is the only poem here to date from the time of, or later
than, the bulk of *The Canterbury Tales*. The poems offered are the
best of Chaucer outside *Troilus and Criseyde* and *The Canterbury
Tales*, both of which are represented in the Penguin Classics, so
that the present work is complementary to that already pub-
lished. These four poems, because of the widely separated dates

of composition, show the development of the poetic art which was fulfilled in the great work by which Chaucer is best known.

With regard to this development, there is some danger of considering Chaucer an isolated phenomenon just because he was the towering genius of his age and country, as Shakespeare was two hundred years later. But of the major poets of his time he was the successful innovator. The great alliterative poets, such as Langland, the poet of *Piers Plowman*, and the authors of *Sir Gawain and the Green Knight* and the alliterative *Morte Arthure*, crowned a dying tradition. But those who, like Chaucer, embraced the French tradition, such as Gower and Lydgate, cannot be compared with our poet. Chaucer was the fourteenth-century English poet who, basing his work on that of his French and Italian peers and also, like them, on the work of classical and late Latin poets, created highly original narrative poems with a skill in story-telling in which he equalled, if not surpassed, his masters. Ovid, whose outlook on women and sense of the great variety of life including the absurd, make him of the ancients most akin to Chaucer, may beat him for sensuousness and richness of detail, and Virgil and Dante for high seriousness and epic scope; but Chaucer offers a subtle humour which enhances the seriousness and complexity of what he has to say, as well as a kaleidoscopic range of tone and subject matter. In this volume, though the source poems which he translated in selection and which he transformed into new artefacts as he part-digested them, are referred to in the Notes, the use he made of them is not discussed in detail. The aim is to encourage enjoyment of the poetry, not study of its sources. Yet, to appreciate Chaucer's achievement, the reader should have some idea of the subject matter he selected for treatment, and some information about the poetic conventions he inherited and worked on. That will be done, as far as the scope of the present volume permits, in the separate introductory essays to the poems, and in the Notes, while a modest list of further reading is offered in the Bibliography.

Now to the main theme of this book, which the title almost fallaciously indicates: 'fallaciously' because on each occasion here (except the first) on which Chaucer ostensibly embarks on what was by convention a poetic ritual, he proceeds by wit and high invention to frustrate ordinary expectation and develop new matters. 'Love vision' was the name given to one sort of poetic expression of the values of courtly love, that rigid system of lofty and mainly aristocratic frivolity into which western European poets were expected to cram both the rich diversity of classical stories and the early medieval inheritance of epic and folklore. The love vision is a dream dreamed by a poet who is in some way ready and yearning to make a discovery about love; either he suffers from love himself or, as in 'The Book of the Duchess' and 'The House of Fame', he falls asleep reading a book which leads him into his dream subject. When the dream begins the poet is often led on by a guide, perhaps into a paradisal park or Garden of Love, where an action or debate about love, most often with allegorical characters and interpretation, takes place. The end comes with the poet-dreamer waking, and bringing from his dream a truth about love as about a sacred mystery. It is a truism that the vocabularies of religious poetry and the poetry of courtly love interpenetrate, and are in some respects, as in the expression of devotion and lofty morality, indistinguishable.

Only the first poem, 'The Book of the Duchess', conforms entirely to this prescription, and even then Chaucer applies to it a winning variation. The poem reaches through the love vision mechanism to an elegy which celebrates the wooing and virtues of a deceased lady and the grief of her lover. The next poem, 'The House of Fame', begins in an orthodox style, with the poet dreaming his way into the Temple of Venus in search of enlightenment about love, and seeing carved or painted illustrations of famous love stories. But from the end of Book I his concern with love is diversified, and the fascination successively of Fame and then Rumour takes over, guided as it is by the earliest of Chaucer's major comic creations, the Eagle. This character starts as a copy of a grand Dantean eagle, but then rapidly reveals himself as a self-satisfied pedant and, as A. W. Ward has it, a 'winged encyclopædia'. The operation of Fame and Rumour are allegorically examined with a humorous intelligence, and just when a conclusive judgement or summing-up of some kind is expected, at the approach of 'a man of great authority' (whom some critics think may be Boethius, others, John of Gaunt, and yet others, some other poet), the poem breaks off, unfinished. We are left with rich ideas about vicissitude in the realms of Love and Fame, and a sense that such a serious matter requires, in the face of centuries-old poetical practice, light and even quizzical treatment. Satire is rarely far from the mind of Chaucer, who is at his best when he probes the complex ambiguities of emotional life.

For the ensuing short and pungent masterpiece, 'The Parliament of Birds' (to which I as translator refuse to give its old and now inaccurate title, 'The Parliament of Fowls'), a special convention of courtly love poetry provides the ostensible framework: the debate among birds, each species pleading a particular attitude to love.* But before we find the birds, assembled at the feet of the goddess Nature, we are offered a lofty pagan sermon about our duty on earth, which is to 'sustain the common good' by our behaviour. Next we are taken on a trip into the paradisal park where allegorical characters mark the way to Venus, lying half-naked; both are narrated in high style, but with enough glints of humour to make us ready for the big surprises which follow. Earthy, commonsensical and utilitarian approaches to love vie successfully with the loftiest – but here, intentionally, not most gracefully expressed – professions of courtly love, and we are left chortling over a humane and realistic synthesis of the subject.

The last poem, 'The Legend of Good Women', is the longest, and the most drastically unfinished, in this book. It starts with a superb Prologue containing some of the loveliest verse Chaucer ever wrote, which introduces his subject, the celebration of Cupid's saints: that is, good women of classical history and myth who were true to love until death. The Prologue is the only part of the work which is technically a love vision. There follow nine legends, containing altogether the stories of ten women. It appears from the Prologue (l.186) that Chaucer may have intended to versify the stories of nineteen, but his ninth story

---

*The English masterpiece in this genre is 'The Owl and the Nightingale' (c.1200), a translation of which also appears in the Penguin classics.

breaks off when apparently needing only a few lines of ending, and there is no conclusion at all to the whole work which, it is thought, was simply abandoned, possibly in favour of the greater creative lure offered by the writing of *The Canterbury Tales*. All but one of the legends – two, if we exculpate Antony – emphasize male perfidy while extolling female virtue. That may sound monotonous, but the variety of tone, ranging from strained, tragic lyricism to almost knockabout satire, and the humorously changing identification of the poet with his subject matter, have not in my view been sufficiently analysed and praised.

The personality of the poet is designedly obtrusive in these poems. The particular persona Chaucer presents in each poem is structural in 'The Book of the Duchess', 'The House of Fame', 'The Parliament of Birds' and the Prologue to 'The Legend of Good Women' in that, without it, the poems could not exist without great impoverishment. In the separate legends, the poet's personality is not integral to the stories although it successfully obtrudes from time to time, especially at the opening or the close of a poem. In 'The Book of the Duchess' the poet is an earnest seeker of relief from love-suffering who, finding one whose pain is greater than his own, adopts a stance of sympathy and naive ignorance in order to draw from the other man some expression of his grief and love, with consolatory effect. In 'The House of Fame', which must count as one of Chaucer's most autobiographical poems, the quest on which he embarks, with its ambiguous non-ending, is a personal one, and the poet – who is almost comically obtuse at times – is accordingly the hero of his own story. This is also true of 'The Parliament of Birds', because we are always aware of the poet-dreamer's judging consciousness; but with less personal effect. In the climax of the poem, the birds' debate and its resolution make such an impact of their own that the return to the awaking poet and his books, in the last lines of the poem, is little more than formal. The Prologue to 'The Legend of Good Women', for all its beautifully fashioned 'vision' apparatus, its famous praise of the daisy and its lyrical intensity, is nevertheless something of an apology by the poet for himself and his work. So in these poems the reader will find, besides the particular delights of each, a poet's self-portrait, by turns ruefully self-deprecatory, self-justifying, psychologically illuminating, often comically responsive to the world he presents and analyses, and always modest, witty and quietly humane.

One development which becomes apparent in presenting four poems in what is assumed to be their chronological order of composition concerns Chaucer's verse forms. He moves from the octosyllabic couplet of French romance, in which 'The Book of the Duchess' and 'The House of Fame' are composed, to rhyme royal in 'The Parliament of Birds'. This is a seven-lined stanza of iambic pentameter, rhyming *ababbcc*, which is so strongly associated with him that it is sometimes called the Chaucerian or Troilus stanza. From rhyme royal, Chaucer turns to the iambic pentameter rhymed couplet of 'The Legend of Good Women', which was to be the basic form of *The Canterbury Tales*. It is used flowingly, without general commitment either to the end-stopped line or the self-contained couplet. Owing to Chaucer, all these forms developed new traditions. The octosyllabic couplet gradually declined in status, and tended to be favoured more for satirical and comic verse, while the iambic pentameter line was to become the characteristic line of English poetry: as blank verse when unrhymed (in the Elizabethan and Stuart plays); as heroic verse when rhymed (in our neo-Classical age); and as the staple length for the line of the sonnet. Chaucer's practice in managing iambic verse is less strict than that of his French masters and English contemporaries. The fluent looseness he sometimes happily adopts, especially in the dropping of the first, unstressed, syllable of a line, was a narrative grace in keeping with an accented language such as English.

The movement in the four poems from allegorical narration to realistic story-telling, as Chaucer gains greater power and more independence from his French and Italian masters, is remarkable. Chaucer is at first rich in settings and descriptions; as P. M. Kean writes in *Love Vision and Debate* (Volume 1 of *Chaucer and the Making of English Poetry*, p.192): 'Since the core of the love vision in French is the didactic speeches, which give instruction concerning Love at length, the descriptions and settings are necessarily subordinate, and there is nothing to compare with Chaucer's thematic use of these parts of his work.' And referring to 'The House of Fame' in particular, she continues: 'It might even be possible to see an element of literary satire in Chaucer's insistence on the elusive love-tidings which are never actually spoken.' The descriptions and settings become less and less set-pieces in Chaucer's later verse narratives, and more and more forcefully integral to the events and people of the tale.

Consequently, the stories become shorter and more realistic, especially after the completion of the great *Troilus and Criseyde*, which is, viewed from a modern standpoint, virtually a romantic novel in verse. Robert Worth Frank, Jr, in a revealing note (*Chaucer and 'The Legend of Good Women'*, pp.8–9), shows that after 'The Knight's Tale' (2,250 lines), which was probably written first of *The Canterbury Tales*, Chaucer 'abandoned the long narrative'. Three of the *Tales* just exceed a thousand lines, but all the rest approximate to the kind of length we find in 'The Legend of Good Women'. In these tales of women who died true to love, Chaucer is nicely selective as his theme requires. The full panoply of the classical story as in Ovid or Virgil is simply not there, and in understanding Chaucer's narrative art the reader cannot do better than compare his story of Dido and Aeneas, which concentrates on the perfidy of the man and the hapless faith of the woman, with Virgil's account in Book IV of the *Aeneid*.

Time and again in his short tales Chaucer leaves out matters which those who know the originals might think essential, until they ponder the reasons for Chaucer's selection. In the last fourteen years of his life he seems to have preferred composing short verse narratives, with highly pertinent description, to other forms of poetry. In *The Canterbury Tales* he was to develop the idea of linking his narratives by fully characterizing the tellers of the stories as members of a whole varied society, and so achieved his masterpiece. In this respect he went beyond other medieval writers who presented collections of tales, such as Boccaccio with his *Decameron* and the author(s) of the Arabian

Thousand and One Nights. 'The Legend of Good Women', the last poem in this book, thus represents the stage Chaucer reached just before starting *The Canterbury Tales*.

Perhaps we should be wary of using the term 'development' too freely. In the very first pages of poetry in this book there is a masterly short story of only 155 lines ('The Book of the Duchess', ll.62–216); the tale of Ceyx and Alcyone expresses irreparable loss of love, and contains descriptions of shipwreck and the Cave of Sleep, besides vivid dialogue of three kinds. Chaucer was always able.

The Book of the Duchess

INTRODUCTION TO
'THE BOOK OF THE DUCHESS'

It is generally accepted that this poem was written for John of
Gaunt after the death of his first wife Blanche in 1369, as the
references towards the end of the poem (see note to l.1318) seem
to make clear. Chaucer, through his wife Philippa, was later to
become the recipient of an annuity from John of Gaunt, and the
Chaucer Life-Records (edited by Crow and Olson, Oxford Univer-
sity Press, 1966) show a continuing connection. That so great a
noble should appear in a poem as a conventional courtly lover –
the knightly Man in Black – should prevent us from expecting
realism in what we read; his actual age and status, and the
historical details of his marriage with Blanche, are scarcely
relevant. The genre Chaucer uses, the love vision, is a meta-
phorical means of achieving the higher reality – in this case,
celebration of a great love and its object, and consolation for the
bereaved lover. Most of the metaphorical items in this celebra-
tion are borrowed by Chaucer from French sources – Machaut
(1300–1377), especially his poem *Le Jugement dou Roy de
Behaingne*, Froissart (?1337–1410) and, of course, *Le Roman de
la Rose*.

Some of the metaphors and other components Chaucer used,
which feature widely in courtly love poetry, in addition to the
dream mechanism described in the general Introduction, may
now be mentioned: the hunt and chess as direct metaphors for
love activity; the telling of another tale (that of Ceyx and
Alcyone) to help set the theme and tone; the spring season and
the singing birds (ll.291–320); the strange formality of the
arrangement of trees in the Garden of Love (ll.414–26); the
physical effect of spiritual suffering (ll.487–513); the polite
conversation throughout; the obtrusive 'colours' of rhetoric (as,
for example, in the list of contraries in ll.599–617); the

extended characterization of fickle Fortune (ll.618–84); the lists of classical parallels; the young man's account of his devotion to Love (l.759 onwards); the description of the loved object, first as a dancer and singer, then as a physical and moral being (ll.815–1041); the falling in love, the suffering; the eventual declaration of love in the form of humble and faithful service (ll.1221–35); and the lady's refusal, followed by years of constancy, before she grants 'mercy', which is here a metaphor for the marriage of John of Gaunt and Blanche.

The story of Ceyx and Alcyone is taken from Ovid (see note to l.63), whom Chaucer draws on for classical material throughout his work, and more often than from any other source. Here, as in 'The Legend of Good Women', Chaucer omits the consolation of the Ovidian metamorphosis of the heroine because it does not suit his theme. In this tale the colloquial speech of Juno and the messenger should not be thought of as a uniquely Chaucerian departure from the tone of his sources. The latter include the French popular *fabliau*, and also Jean de Meun's continuation of *Le Roman de la Rose*, in which frank and often crude ordinary speech (but presented in verse) is the rule for certain allegorical characters. Chaucer's debt to this element in French poetry remained constant: a famous exemplar is the Wife of Bath, whose speeches are exactly like those of Jean de Meun's Duenna, who is quoted directly more than once.

The grand movement of the poem must now be traced. The true action begins with the appearance of the Man in Black (l.445), his long and passionate outpouring, and the Dreamer's response (l.710). All before that is thematic preparation: the poet's sleeplessness as he nurses an undefined sorrow, the 'exquisite relevance of the Ceyx and Alcyone story' (Muscatine, *Chaucer and the French Tradition*, p.102), and the anticipatory immersion in the dream world of Love. When the poet's exclamation (ll.240–69) works in the real life of the poem exactly as Alcyone's prayer to Juno works in the story – that is, he is granted the gift of sleep – we are aware of a humorous sophistication, which guards the modesty of the Poet when he subsequently consoles a great noble for his loss – and with apparent success.

His first response to the Man in Black's grief is a philosophical, Boethian one; it could also be called Christian counsel in the form of a warning against immoderate grief. Critics have sometimes expressed puzzlement that the Poet knows, from line 491 onwards, that Blanche is dead, and yet, when the Man in Black can finally state it at line 1309, he pretends to hear it for the first time. That is to fail to appreciate the major sophistication of the poem, which is to set up the ideal frame for the expression of its important content. Only if the Poet, relying on the Man in Black's assumption of his ignorance, can draw forth happy memories of the loved one now dead, can there be any consoling effect – though even that will be limited, as the abrupt ending of the poem implies.

The poet performs this drawing forth by explicit request (ll. 746–8), having won the Man in Black's confidence. The lyricism of the sorrower's recall acts as a kind of balm. But that first outpouring of love, which ends at line 1041, does not express either the progress of the love affair or its ending; these have to be provoked by the Poet's successive questions, each of which, surprising to the Man in Black by its deliberate provocation, requires a vigorous riposte. The last provocation, 'Where is she now?' (l. 1298), would have been unforgivable if the Knight had thought the Poet already knew Blanche was dead. As it is, the 'revelation' can be responded to by the Poet with a full heart. Then since consolation, the easing of true grief, can only be temporary, no more can be said:

> ... all was done
> That day in hunting of the hart.

The felicitous pun (heart/hart) completes the action, and the whole poem must end with the identification of the protagonist and the waking of the dreamer.

(Useful criticism and notes on the French sources and analogies may be found in the scholarly edition just published: Helen Phillips (ed.), *Chaucer: The Book of the Duchess*, Durham and St Andrew's Medieval Texts, 1982.)

THE BOOK OF THE DUCHESS

By heaven above, I wonder much
I stay alive, my sleep is such
By night and day – the barest wink!
So many useless thoughts I think,
Simply through lack of sleep and rest,
That nothing stirs my mind or breast.
Indifferent to what comes or goes,
I harbour neither joys nor woes.
Love or hate, whichever it be,
Brings equal profit now to me.   10
In spirit and sensation numb,
I'm spellbound in a trance and dumb,
Likely at any time to fall;
For dreary speculations gall
And ever dominate my mind.
   Against the laws of humankind
It is to stay in such a mood,
For nature does not count it good
For any living being on earth
To suffer long devoid of mirth   20
And sleepless, lapped in grief and sorrow.
And truly, night and noon and morrow
I cannot sleep; a heavy gloom
So threatens me with thoughts of doom.
This lack of sleep and sluggishness
Have so destroyed my liveliness
That I have lost all energy.
Such weird imaginings come to me
I don't know what is for the best.

Men ask me why I cannot rest, 30
And wonder what my trouble is;
But all the same, whoever asks this
Inquires in vain, for even I
Myself can't tell the reason why
In truth; but really it must be,
As I suppose, the malady
That I have suffered for eight years.*
As yet, no cure for it appears.
As for physicians, only one
Can heal me; and that hope is gone. 40
So let us leave what can't be cured
Till later; it must be endured,
And to our story we must keep.

So when I found I could not sleep
Though it was late, one special night
I sat upon my bed upright
And asked my man to fetch a book
Of old romance, which then I took
To read, to drive the night away –
Which seemed a better game to play 50
Than chess, backgammon or other sport.

This book contained the storied thought
Of learned men of olden time
And poets who composed in rhyme
For men in tune with nature's law,
To read and mind it evermore.
Its tales were wholly of such things
As lives of queens and lives of kings,
And lesser things of many a kind,
Among all which I chanced to find 60
What seemed to me a marvellous thing.

This was the tale: there was a king
Whose name was Ceyx.* He took a wife,
The best that ever breathed in life,
And this was Queen Alcyone.
The marriage made, immediately
The King must needs go oversea.

To make this part a brevity,
When he was launched upon the ocean,
A tempest came with huge commotion   70
And broke the mast and made it fall,
And split the ship and drowned them all.
And none were found, the story tells –
Not planks, not men, nor one thing else.
And so King Ceyx had lost his life.
   Now speak we of the Queen, his wife.
This lady, who was left at home,
Perplexed her husband did not come
Though his due date was long since past,
With grief of spirit was downcast.   80
His absence filled her with alarm;
It meant, she thought, he'd come to harm.
Her longing for the King was such
That truly it would pain me much
To tell the sorrowful, grieving life
Then suffered by this noble wife
For him she loved of all the best.
At once she sent forth east and west
In search, but always was denied.
'Alas that I was born!' she cried,   90
'Suppose my Lord, my love, is dead?
I swear I never will take bread
Till I hear something of my love:
I pledge this oath to God above!'
Such dreadful grief this lady took
That truly I who write this book
Felt such a powerful sympathy
At reading her calamity
That I felt ill upon the morrow,
Pondering her heavy sorrow.   100
   So when this lady heard no word
Of any kind about her lord,
She cried, 'Alas!' and swooned and pined;
With grief she almost lost her mind.
One course alone could do her ease:

In tears she went down on her knees
And wept aloud most sad to hear.
   'Have mercy on me, Lady dear!'
She prayed to Juno,* her goddess,
'Deliver me from my distress,   110
And grant me soon the grace to see
My Lord, or know where he may be;
What chance is his, its hows and whys,
And I shall do you sacrifice,
And I'll be yours, entire and whole
In body, spirit, heart and soul.
And if, sweet Lady, you esteem
My prayer, then grant me grace to dream,
When next I sleep, a dream that so
Through it I may for certain know   120
Whether my Lord's alive or dead.'
   And with that word she bowed her head
And fainted, cold as any stone.
Her women caught her in her swoon
And laid her naked in her bed,
And there, worn out with tears and dread,
She unawares gave way to a deep
And seemingly a lifeless sleep.
For Juno, who had heard her prayer,
Thus gave her sleep so quickly there,   130
And as she prayed, it was fulfilled.
The goddess Juno swiftly willed
It so and called her messenger
To do her errand. He came to her
And she at once commanded thus:
'Go hurry now to Morpheus,*
The god of sleep, you know him well.
Now mark me closely. Go and tell
Him absolutely as from me
To speed into the mighty sea,   140
Come what may, with no delays,
And find the corpse of good King Ceyx,
Which lies there pale, not live and ruddy.

Tell him to creep into the body
And take it where in lonely dread
The Queen Alcyone lies in bed,
And tell her in the plainest way
How it was drowned that fateful day;
And make the body give tongue too
Exactly as it used to do   150
When Ceyx the King was a living man.
Now go as quickly as you can!'
The messenger bade farewell in haste.
Without a pause the fellow raced
Until he came to that grim dale
Between two rocks, a gloomy vale
Where never yet grew tree or grain
Or grass, and all growth was in vain –
No man, no beast, no living thing,
Except that here and there a spring   160
Flowed with a deadly sleepy sound
Down from the cliffs that reared around;
Flowed down beside a yawning cave
Beneath a carven rock which gave
Upon the valley dark and deep.
And there those gods lay fast asleep,
Morpheus, and Enclimpostair*
Who was the God of Slumber's heir.
They slept and did no other work.
That cave was gloomy too, as dark   170
All round as pit of hell and more.
They had good leisure there to snore,
Contending who could sleep the best.
Some hung the chin upon the breast
And slept upright with covered head,
And some lay naked in their bed
And slept as long as day might last.
    This messenger came flying fast
And cried, 'What ho! Wake up! Give ear!'
No use. They simply did not hear.   180
'Wake up!' said he, 'Who's lying there?'

26

And blew his horn right in their ear,
Shouting, 'Wake up!' with piercing cry.
This god of sleep with just one eye
Looked up and asked, 'Who's calling there?'
'I am!' replied the messenger.
'Juno commands you now to go –'
And told him what he had to do
Exactly as I said before:
I shan't repeat it any more!   190
And having said his say, departed.
At once the God of Slumber started
Swiftly from deepest sleep to go
And do as she had bid him do;
Picked up the drowned corpse speedily
And bore it to Alcyone
The Queen his consort where she lay,
Three hours before the break of day.
There to the bed's foot then he came,
And calling to her by her name   200
Said this to her, 'My own sweet wife,
Awake! Forsake your grieving life!
For since I am but dead, in brief,
There lies no profit in your grief,
For you shall never see me more
Alive. So, sweetest heart, therefore
Bury my body lovingly
Whenever you find it by the sea.
Adieu, my sweet, my earthly bliss!
Pray God may heal your grief at this!   210
Our joy on earth is all too short!'
    At that she raised her eyes and sought
Him vainly. 'Woe, alas!' she cried,
And on the third day after, died.
I shall not tell what else she said
Before her swooning laid her dead –
Too long a matter on which to dwell.
But back to my original tale:
The reason why I told this thing

Of Alcyone and Ceyx the King.   220
  For this much dare I say to you,
I should be dead and buried too
Through utter lack of sleep and rest
Had I not read and been impressed
By the tale I've told you. I
Shall now proceed to tell you why,
Since truly, neither joy nor dread
Could make me sleep till I had read
Of Ceyx's drowning in the deep,
And also of the gods of sleep.   230
When I had taken it to heart
And pondered over every part,
I wondered much if it were true,
For until then I never knew
Of any gods with power to make
Men fall asleep or start awake.
But then, of gods I knew but one.
So I exclaimed, almost in fun,
Although my mood was far from jest,
'Rather than be without my rest   240
And die for lack of slumber thus,
I'd offer to that Morpheus –
Or Lady Juno, his goddess,
Or any other, more or less –
To make me sleep and have some rest –
I'd give to him the very best
Present that ever he did receive,
And here, at once, you must believe,
If he will close my eyes in sleep:
A feather-bed both wide and deep   250
Of softest down from pure white dove,
With stripes of gold and hung above
With fine black satin from oversea,
And many a pillow, cased, marked me,
In linen of Rennes* of softest floss
For sleep. No need to turn and toss!
I'd give him furnishings for all

His bedroom needs; and every hall
Of his I'd paint with purest gold.
He should have tapestries many-fold   260
In matching hues. These should he have
If I knew where to find his cave,
If sleep he'd quickly give to me
As Juno did to Alcyone.
Thus Morpheus would earn from me
As thanks the most substantial fee
He ever won. To Juno too,
His goddess, I would offer due
Observance to her just content.'

   To this I'd scarcely given vent   270
Exactly as I tell you now,
When suddenly, I know not how,
Such longing to be fast asleep
Assailed me that I sank down deep
In slumber on my open book.
At once a marvellous vision took
My dreaming mind, so sweet that it
Would be beyond a wise man's wit
To give it right interpretation.
Not Joseph of old Egypt's nation,   280
Interpreter of Pharaoh's dream,*
Could read it rightly, as I deem,
Or better than the least of us.
Indeed, not even Macrobius*
(He whose vision made him know
The dreams of great King Scipio,
The African, to whom there came
Such fateful marvels and such fame)
Could read my dream with insight clear;
This dream of mine you now shall hear.   290

   It seemed to me that it was May,
And in the dawn I sleeping lay,
When I was roused from naked bed,
Was woken up and raised my head,
Because small birds in countless number

Had sweetly startled me from slumber
With all their din of morning song.
And, so I dreamed, they perched along
My bedroom roof and all about
Upon the tiles, each singing out   300
In solemn individual note
More splendid matins from its throat
Than ever man had heard, I know.
For some sang high and some sang low,
Making harmonious accord.
To tell you briefly, in a word,
So sweet a song was never heard –
Except, of course, from heavenly bird.
Such blissful sound, such lovely tunes
That I'd forgo the town of Tunis*   310
For joy of listening to them sing!
For all my room began to ring
With sound of their sung harmony.
No instrument or melody
In tune or concord of sweet sound
Of half such bliss was ever found.
Not one of those birds feigned to sing,
For all were raptly fostering
Discovery of lovely notes.
They did not spare their tuneful throats.   320
To tell the truth my chamber was
Adorned with pictures, while with glass
Were all the windows glazed and clear;
And not a single hole was there,
So that to see it was great joy.
For truly all the tale of Troy
Was in the glass depicted thus;
Of Hector and King Priamus,*
Achilles and Laomedon,
Medea and Jason, Aeson's son,   330
Lavinia, Paris and Helen too;
And on the walls in varied hue
Was painted, with its text and gloss,

All *The Romance of the Rose*.
My windows there were closed each one,
And through the panes the bright sun shone
Upon my bed in glittering streams
Of merrily shimmering golden gleams.
And all the heaven above was fair,
Sky blue and bright, and clear the air;   340
Yet temperate was the weather, not
Too chilly cold nor yet too hot,
And all the welkin clear of cloud.

   And as I lay thus, very loud
It seemed I heard a huntsman blow
To test his horn and so to know
Whether its call were clogged or clear.
Comings and goings I could hear,
Men, horse and hounds in every place,
And all men talking of the chase: 350
How they would run the hart to death
And how the hart, quite out of breath
And sweating at last – I know not what!
The moment that I heard all that,
And knew it was a hunting day,
My heart rejoiced, and straight away
I left my room and on my horse
Went prancing forth without a pause
Until I reached the hunting field,
On which a crowd of horsemen wheeled,   360
Huntsmen and foresters renowned,
With sets of deer- and tracker-hound.
Fast to the forest then they ran
And I with them. I asked a man
Who led a pack of deer-hounds there,
'Whose are these fine huntsmen here?'
And civilly he answered, 'Sir,
Octavian the Emperor,*
And he himself is fast nearby.'
'Well met, by God! Let's hurry,' said I.   370
And swiftly then did we two ride

31

Until we reached the forest side.
There every man was doing just
As he by laws of hunting must.
Three long notes blew the master then
Upon his great horn, telling men
To unleash and urge on every hound.
And quickly then the hart was found,
Hallooed and keenly hunted fast
Long time with shouts; until at last   380
The hart zigzagged and stole away
From all the hounds a secret way.
The pack entire thus overshot
And lost the scent they'd had so hot.
At once the master-huntsman knew,
And on his horn the recall blew.
   I had been posted by a tree,
And when I left it, came to me
A pup that fawned and followed close,
Not knowing what a deer-hound knows.   390
And fawning so, it crawled before me
As if it knew me when it saw me,
Lowering its head with flattened ears
And smoothing down its bristling hairs.
I would have caught it, but it fled
Away from me and dashed ahead.
I followed it, and off it scoured
Along a pathway green and flowered
And thick with grass and blossoms sweet,
Delightful to my treading feet.   400
It seemed the path had little use
And that Flora and Zephyrus,*
The two that give the flowers growth,
Were dwelling in it, by my troth.
And as I looked, it was as though
The earth were trying to outdo
And be more beautiful than heaven,
To have more flowers, seven times seven,
Than there are bright stars in the sky.

The winter's dearth it had put by,   410
The rigours of the icy morrow,
The suffering, the time of sorrow:
All was forgotten, as was seen,
For all the wood was bright with green.
Sweetness of dew had made it grow.
No need to ask, because you know,
Whether green groves were on that ground
Or leafy thickets were all around.
Yet every tree stood ten or twelve
Feet from another, by itself.   420
Great trees they were in size and might,
Rearing eighty feet in height
Devoid of bough or branch or twig,
Then broad at top, so thick and big,
The branches not an inch asunder,
That everywhere was shadow under.
And many a hart and many a hind
Were there before me and behind.
Of fawns, bucks young and old, and does,
The wood was full, with many roes,   430
And many squirrels too that sat
Aloft upon the trees and ate,
Making their special kinds of feasts.
In short, it was so full of beasts
That Algus,* nimble-fingered clerk
In his counting-house at work
Reckoning with his one to ten –
Those figures which calculating men
If they are clever, can use to tell
And number all things very well –   440
I say even Algus could not number
The marvels of my dreaming slumber.
  The roaming creatures galloped fast
About the forest; then at last
I suddenly saw a man in black
Reclining seated with his back
Against an oak, a giant tree.

'Oh Lord!' thought I, 'who can he be?
What fortune dogs him, sitting here?'
And straight away, as I drew near,   450
I saw the seated man was quite
A splendidly good-looking knight –
His stately manner told me so –
Of noble stature, youthful too,
Say, four and twenty years of age,*
Not bushy-bearded at this stage:
And he was wholly clad in black.
I tiptoed quietly towards his back,
Then stood stock-still; and in a word,
Me he neither saw nor heard,   460
Because he hung his head and sighed,
And with a deathly mourning cried
A rhyme of verses ten or twelve
In lamentation to himself
More pitiful and charged with woe
Than ever I had heard. I know
It seemed remarkable that Nature
Could suffer any living creature
To bear such grief and not be dead.
Most sadly pale, not white and red,   470
He spoke a lyric, a kind of song,
Yet tune thereto did not belong.
It started thus, for every word
I can recall just as I heard:

'In deepest sorrow I am thrown;
Joys and pleasures have I none
Now that I know my Lady bright,
Whom I have loved with all my might,
Is far from me, and dead and gone.*   479
What ails you, Death, what misery .   481
You did not wish to capture me
When yet you stole my Lady dear,
Who was so fine and nobly free,

So good that everyone could see
In virtue she possessed no peer?'

When he had ended his complaint
His grieving heart began to faint,
His spirit to flag as it were dead,
And all his blood for very dread   490
Suffused his heart to make it warm.
Blood knew the heart had come to harm
And was afraid; by natural art
It wished to cheer the grieving heart,
For heart is body's member-in-chief.
That rush of blood to cure its grief
Had left the knight's complexion green
And pale because no blood was seen
In any feature he possessed.
At once, perceiving him oppressed   500
And sitting there in state so grim,
I went and stood in front of him
And greeted him. He answered not,
Being wrapped up in his inward thought,
Considering keenly how and why
His misery had not made him die;
So sharp his sorrows manifold,
They lay upon his heart ice-cold.
And thus his woes and gloomy thought
So weighed on him he heard me not.   510
He'd almost lost his sanity,
However furious Pan* might be,
The God of Nature, at his grief.
    But finally, to my relief,
He did perceive me where I stood
Before him taking off my hood,
Saluting him as best I could,
Politely, not uncouth and loud.
'I pray do not be cross,' said he,
'I did not hear you, honestly,   520

35

Nor did I see you.' 'Sir,' I said,
'No matter, trouble not your head.
And I for my part much regret
If anything I did upset
Your train of thought. Forgive me, please!'
'That I do,' said he, 'with ease.
To make amends there is no need,
For nothing's wrong in word or deed.'
Behold! How kindly spoke this knight,
As if a different person quite,   530
Without false style or sense of rank;
Seeing which, I felt that he was frank,
And found him most approachable,
And very wise and reasonable,
For so he seemed despite his woe.
And then I found a way to go
Closer in thought to him and find
What troubled him and pained his mind.
I said, 'The chase is done, I say!
I think this hart is gone away: 540
The hunt can't find him anywhere.'
Replied the knight, 'I do not care;
I give it not a single thought.'
'I well believe it, by Our Lord,'
I said, 'I see it in your face.
But let me, sir, present a case.
It seems I see you in great woe,
But if, Sir Knight, you let me know
The cause of this tremendous ill,
As sure as God gives help, I will,   550
If power is granted me, remove it.
Your trying me will let me prove it,
For by my troth, to put you right
I shall put forth my utmost might.
So tell me of your bitter grief;
For that may give your heart relief,
That heart which pains you in your side.'
At that he rather glanced aside

As if to say, 'That cannot be.'
'I thank you, gentle friend,' said he,   560
'Sincerely for your kind intent,
But that will not my grief prevent.
No man can cheer my utter woe,
Which pales my natural colours so,
And makes my spirit so forlorn
I wish that I had not been born.
Not all of Ovid's Remedies,*
Nor Orpheus with his melodies,
Nor Daedalus with his crafty brain,
Could smooth away my sorrow's pain.   570
Not Galen nor Hippocrates
Could heal my woe or do me ease.
I grieve that I live half a day!
Let any man who will, essay,
If pity for others' grief may be
Within his heart, to look on me!
O wretched me, whom Death stripped clean
Of all the bliss that's ever been!
Become unluckiest of knights,
Detesting all my days and nights!   580
I hate delights and joy in life;
With all well-being I'm at strife.
Yes, Death himself's so much my foe:
I'd die, but he won't have it so.
For when I seek him, he will flee;
I'd have him, but he won't have me.
This is my chronic pain and dread,
Always dying without being dead,
So bad that Sisyphus* in hell
Cannot of greater sorrow tell.   590
Sure any man who understood
My catalogue of sorrows would
A fiend-like heart and soul possess
Unless he pitied my distress.
A man who sees me any morrow
Can say that he has met with sorrow,

37

For I am sorrow, and sorrow is I.
   'Alas! and I shall tell you why.
My merry song's now plaintive singing;
My laughter's changed to tears' stinging,   600
My happy musings to distress,
My cheerful work to idleness.
My rest is work, my weal is woe;
My good is harm, my pleasures go
In endless rage, while happiness
Converts in me to joylessness.
My health is sickness out and out,
And all my certainty is doubt.
Turned to dark is all my light.
My wit is folly, my day, night;   610
My sleep is waking, my love, hate;
My mirth and meat are in famished state.
My confidence departed, I
Am everywhere abashed and shy.
Trouble and strife abuse my peace:
How could things be worse than this?
My boldness is timidity,
For fickle Fortune plays with me
A game of chess, alas the while!
That traitress, false and full of guile,   620
Whose promise is not worth the name,
Who walks erect and yet is lame,
Who foully squints and yet looks fair,
Disdainful and yet debonair,
Despised by many and many a creature;
An idol artists falsely feature,
For being a ghoul's head in disguise,
She offers change and foul surprise,
Like ordure covered up with flowers.
Her chief renown in treacherous powers   630
Is lying with instinctive force;
For, faithless, lawless, all recourse
To truth denied, she has one eye
In mirth, and one with tears awry.

What is set up, she will cast down.
I liken her to the scorpion,
A false and flattering kind of beast,
For with his head he makes a feast
Of fawning, in which toadying
His tail flicks out a baneful sting   640
Most venomous, and so does she.
She is the rancorous charity
Who seems to offer good with zeal,
But ever false, her treacherous wheel
She turns, and never leaves it stable,
Not by fireside nor at table.
For she has blinded many thus,
Being made of practice sorcerous,
Seeming one thing, not being that.
False thief! What trickery was she at,   650
D'you think? By heaven, I'll tell you, yes!
She came to play with me at chess.
With various moves unfair and mean
She stole on me and took my queen.
And when I saw my queen had gone,
Alas! No more could I play on,
But cried, "Farewell, my sweet! and sure,
Farewell to all for evermore!"
And Fortune then cried, "Check!" in scorn
And "Mate!" She had advanced a pawn   660
To mid-point of the board, alas!
A craftier player of chess she was
Than Attalus* (that was his name)
Who was the inventor of the game.
But would to God I'd been aware
Of all the problems that there were,
As was the Greek Pythagoras!*
I should have played the better at chess,
And better kept my queen thereby.
And yet wherefore? For truly I   670
Esteem that wish not worth a straw;
I'd not have made a better draw.

For Fortune's tricks come thick and fast,
And few can beat her down at last.
And truly she is not to blame;
Myself I'd surely do the same,
By God, were I composed as she;
And thus from blame she should be free.
And furthermore, I'll say this too:
Had I been God, with power to do   680
My will, when Fortune took my queen,
My move would just the same have been.
As sure as God will grant me rest,
I swear she took the very best.
But through that move my bliss is gone:
Alas the day that I was born!
My joy is lost for evermore,
Despite my wishes, I am sure.
So what is to be done? ask I.
By God! It is — at once to die.   690
There's nothing I believe, in short,
But life and death in this one thought.
No planet in the firmament,
In air and earth no element,
But offers me a gift each one
Of weeping when I'm all alone.
For when I think it out with care,
Considering all things here and there,
I see the reckoning does not owe
Me anything in the way of woe,   700
And there exists no happiness
To gladden me in my distress;
And since content is vanished quite,
It follows I have no delight,
And say that I have nothing left.
So thinking I am thus bereft,
Alas! then I am overcome!
For what is done is not to come.
I have more woes than Tantalus.'*
    And when I heard him grieving thus,   710

As I relate, with all that pain,
I felt I hardly could remain,
It filled my heart with so much woe.
'Good sir,' I answered, 'say not so!
Take pity on your nature true
That made a creature out of you.
Remember Socrates* because
He did not count it worth three straws,
Whatever Fortune brought about.'
Said he, 'I cannot: that is out.'   720
'Why so?' I asked. 'By God, good sir,
Don't say, "That's out", for I aver
That if you'd lost all pieces twelve,
And out of grief had killed yourself,
You'd be condemned with just such right
As was Medea,* who killed in spite
Her young by Jason, Aeson's son,
Or Phyllis who for Demophon
Hanged herself – alas the day! –
Because he stayed too long away.   730
And Dido, Queen of Carthage, too,
When out of mind with passion, slew
Herself because Aeneas betrayed her.
What a fool that action made her!
And when Narcissus would not love her,
Echo* died; and others, moreover,
Performed like follies far and wide;
Like Samson* who for Delilah died,
Crushed to death by a pillar's weight.
But no one now would be prostrate   740
With grief because he lost his queen.'
    'Why not?' he asked. 'You cannot mean
What you have said: my cause of woe
Is worse than you can ever know.'
'Ye gods! How could it be?' said I.
'Tell me, good sir, the how and why
And wherefore, all the tale's distress,
Of how you lost your happiness.'

'Delighted! Come, sit down,' said he.
'I'll tell you all if you agree   750
To concentrate on hearing it
With diligence and all your wit.'
'I do, sir.' 'Swear it with an oath!'
'Gladly.' 'Plight your utmost troth!'
'God save me, sir! I shall with joy
My undivided wit employ,
And hear you out as best I can.'
Said he, 'In God's name!' and began:
'Good sir, since first I felt my mind*
In youth to wit and sense inclined;   760
Since first my nature and compassion
Could comprehend in any fashion
What love might be, beyond all doubt
I have most faithfully throughout
Paid tribute as a devotee
To Love most unrestrainedly,
And joyfully become his thrall
With willing body, heart and all.
I served him thus with full accord
And did him homage as my lord.   770
I prayed to him devotedly
So to dispose my heart that he
Should gain from it delightful cheer,
With honour to my Lady dear.
    'For ages, many and many a year
Before my heart served anywhere,
I carried on thus unaware,
As Nature ruled, I do declare.
Perhaps I was most fit for that,
Like a white wall or table flat,   780
Which is most apt to catch and take
Whatever image man may make,
Painted or drawn with all his guile,
No matter how involved the style.
And all that time, though so concerned
With love, I found I worked and learned

Perhaps as much of other matters
Such as science, art and letters;
But love being foremost in my thought,
It was a thing I never forgot.   790
I chose love as my primal skill,
And therefore it is with me still,
Because I learned it at an age
So tender that no spiteful rage
Could then destroy my feeling heart
With too much knowledge of love's art.
For in those days my mistress Youth
Ruled me with idleness in truth;
For it was early youth with me,
And little goodness could I see.   800
Thenceforth my deeds in lightness grew,
And all my thoughts were wayward too;
All things to me alike were good
That then I knew: so matters stood.
    'I chanced upon a place one day*
Where I beheld, I truly say,
The loveliest troop of ladies bright
That ever human being with sight
Had found together in one place.
Now shall I call it chance or grace   810
That took me there? Neither, alas!
Fortune the practised liar it was,
The traitress, faithless and perverse.
Would God that I could call her worse!
For she torments me fiercely now,
And I shall quickly tell you how.
    'Among these ladies fair and bright,
Truly one there struck my sight,
Unlike the others, I declare,
Because for certain I can swear   820
That, as the sun of summer bright
Is fairer, clearer, has more light
Than any other planet in heaven,
More than the Moon, or the starry seven,*

Just so for all the world did she
Surpass those others utterly
In beauty, courtesy and grace,
In radiant modesty of face,
Fine bearing, virtue every way –
What more, thus briefly, can I say?   830
By Christ and his apostles twelve,
It was my sweet, her right true self –
Demeanour steadfast, calm and free,
And poise imbued with dignity.
And Love, who well had heard my prayer,
Had answered me so quickly there
That she at once was wholly caught,
So help me God, within my thought;
So suddenly that then I took
Advice from nothing but her look   840
And my own heart. So since her eyes
Noticed my heart, as I surmise,
I felt in my own mind assured:
Better serve her without reward
Than serve another and be loved well.
And that proved true; and I shall tell
You now the detailed history.
   'I saw her dance so gracefully,
Ring-dancing and most sweetly singing,
Her womanly laughter gaily ringing,   850
Her glances full of graciousness,
Her voice so warm with kindliness,
That never was there seen, I aver,
A treasure-house of bliss like her.
For every hair upon her head,
To state it truly, was not red,
Nor yellow, nor yet brown in hue,
But glittering golden to the view.
And what eyes my Lady had!
Gentle and good, steadfast yet glad,   860
Open, fair-sized, not set too wide.
She did not slyly glance aside,

But openly with candid mien
She gazed on all that could be seen,
And on those who beheld her too.
   'Those eyes might give, in some men's view
A hope of mercy – so fools thought;
But she was not so simply sought.
And this was nothing counterfeit;
Her own pure glance, the cause of it,   870
Was made by Nature, the goddess,
Open and free of artfulness,
Yet circumspect. Whatever bliss
Might take her, she showed no remiss
Or wanton looks, though full of glee.
But ever her eye declared to me,
"If I show wrath, may God forgive!"
   'It pleased her thus so well to live
That dullness slunk in dread away.
Being not too grave and not too gay,   880
She had in all more moderation
Than other ladies in creation.
But with her look she made men smart,
And that sat lightly on her heart
Because she did not know their woe;
And whether she knew or did not know,
In any case she felt no care.
No man could get her love, I swear,
Who dwelled at home here or in Ind;
The nearest was the least in mind.   890
But virtuous folk above all others
She loved, as good men love their brothers,
And gave such love with fine largess
At fit times in all seemliness.
But what a face my Lady had!
Alas! my heart is sorely sad
I cannot give account of it!
.I lack the English and the wit
To tell its loveliness in full;
Besides, my spirit is too dull   900

To grasp so great a thing entire.
I have no wit that can aspire
To comprehend her loveliness.
But she – and this I can but stress –
Was pink and white, fresh, lively-hued,
And daily her beauty was renewed.
Her face was best, in highest measure,
For truly, Nature took such pleasure
To make it lovely that she might
Be the ideal of beauty bright,   910
Highest example of Nature's work
And paragon: in deepest dark
I seem to see her evermore.
To all those things add this: restore
To life all who were once alive,
Not one of all those could contrive
To find foul evil in her face,
For it was grave and full of grace.
  'And what low-toned and gentle speech
Had that sweet one, my life's own leech!   920
So friendly and so firmly grounded,
Upon all reason rightly founded,
And so inclinable to good
That I can swear upon the Rood
So sweet a sounding eloquence
Was never found so full of sense,
So true of tongue, so free of scorn,
So prompt to heal. I dare be sworn
The Mass when by the high Pope sung
Would be as likely as her tongue   930
To cause a man or woman harm.
For hurt in her was hid in balm –
She would not speak in flattery
But, uttering pure simplicity,
Made statements firm as oaths that bind,
Or pledges by a true hand signed.
She never could be pressed to chide;
And that is known of her world-wide.

'That sweet one's neck was so well graced   940
That every bone was rightly placed,
And not a blemish could be seen.
White, smooth and straight it was; lines clean,
No hollows showing, collar-bone,
To all appearance, had she none.
Her throat, as it comes back to me,
Seemed a round tower of ivory,
Shapely and middle-sized, I swear.
  'Her name, it was good Blanche the Fair.*
That was my Lady's name, most right
Because she was both fair and bright;   950
Her birth-name surely was not wrong!
Most lovely shoulders, body long
And arms, like every limb, God knows,
Well clothed with flesh, but nothing gross.
White hands she had; her nails were red,
Her breasts were round, her hips well-bred,
And lovely was her straight flat back.
I knew in her no single lack,
For all, as far as I could tell,
In every part was fashioned well.   960
  'And she could be so blithe and gay
When so inclined, that I can say
That she was like a torch so bright
That everyone could take its light
Yet never make that light the less.
In manners and in comeliness
Just so my Lady did appear;
And all could take from her fine cheer
Enough to make their spirits stir
If they had eyes to look at her.   970
For I dare swear if she had been
Among ten thousand beauties seen,
She would have been at very least
The chiefest mirror at the feast,
Though all were standing in a row,
For men whose eyes could judge and know.

A sociable or festive throng
Without her presence seemed as wrong,
As naked, I could see at once,
As crown not set with precious stones.   980
To my eyes then – with truth I speak –
She was the Arabian bird unique,
The Phoenix.* Single in beauty so,
She had no equal that I know.

   'Now as for goodness, truly she
Had as much fine courtesy
As Esther* in the Bible or,
If that were possible, even more.
Beside that liberal virtue went
A spirit so intelligent,   990
Inclined so wholly to all good,
She set her genius, by the Rood,
Devoid of malice, on delight.
She never did an act of spite;
I never knew such innocence.
I do not say she had no sense
Of evil: otherwise she would
Have known much less about the good.

   'As for good faith, I do declare,
If she had none, a pity it were.   1000
Indeed, so generous was her share,
As I most confidently swear,
That Truth himself had built his hall
In her, his residence principal
By choice, to make his resting-place.
Therefore she had such utter grace
In having steadfast constancy
And self-control both mild and free,
I never knew the like of it,
So purely tolerant her wit.   1010
Reason with joy she understood –
It followed well that she knew good;
She used most gladly to do well.
Thus did her grace in all excel.

48

'She loved the right so keenly too,
No wrong to any would she do;
And none could do her any shame,
So well she guarded her good name.
She gave no false encouragement,*
Nor did she ever with intent   1020
Half promise men to do them grace
By an ambiguous word or face,
Though men might tell such lies of her;
Nor send men to Wallachia,
To Tartary or Prussia,
Turkey or Alexandria;
Nor send one hoodless without delay
To the Gobi Desert far away,
And by the Black Lake make return,
Saying, "Sir, be your concern   1030
That here I may speak well of you,
Till you come back with honour due."
She spurned such petty artifice.
    'But why do I go on like this?
On this same beauty I have said
My love was altogether laid;
To me that flower of womanhood
Was life and joy and source of good,
Fortune, well-being, utter bliss,
Profit on earth, and my goddess.   1040
And I belonged to her entire.'
    I said, 'I well believe you, sire.
You chose right well. I fail to see
How you could choose a better she.'
'Better? None did so well,' said he.
'By God!' said I, 'I do agree!'
'And so you should!' 'Indeed I do.
I stand on my belief that you
Considered that she was the best,
And to behold the loveliest   1050
If seen through your eyes only, sir.'
'Through mine? No, all who looked on her

49

Affirmed and swore that it was true,
And had they had a different view,
I'd still have loved my Lady best,
Yes, even though I had possessed
The beauty of Alcibiades,*
And all the strength of Hercules,
And Alexander's excellence,
And all the wealth and affluence   1060
That ever was in Babylon,
In Carthage or in Macedon,
Or Rome, or Nineveh of old.
Or had I been as brave and bold
As Hector was – may I have joy! –
Whom Achilles killed at Troy
(For that Achilles perished too,
When in Apollo's temple two
Were slain, he and Archilochus,
For so says Dares Phrygius:*   1070
Love of Polyxena the cause),
Or been as wise as Minerva* was,
I'd still have loved her just as much
Eternally, my need being such.
"Need!" I prattle idly now!
There was none, and I'll tell you how.
For my heart freely wished it so,
And I was bound my love to show
As to the fairest and the best.
She was as good – may my soul rest! –   1080
As was Penelope of Greece,*
Or as that noble wife, Lucrece,
Who was the best – he tells it us,
The Roman, Titus Livius.*
She was as good, but not the same,
Though both their stories have just fame.
Yet Blanche, like her, was loyal and true.
   'But why do I relate to you
When first I saw my Lady fair?
Quite young I was, I do declare,   1090

And great need had I then to learn;
So when my heart was set to yearn
With love, it was a mighty quest.
I used my wit as I could best,
As far as childish sense permitted,
And fearlessly I then committed
My spirit to love her loftily,
To do her honour and faithfully
To serve as truly as I could:
Not false, not lax, but firm and good.   1100
Most fervently I longed to see
My sweet: so well she physicked me
That when I saw her any morrow,
I was cured of all my sorrow
That whole long day until the eve;
I felt that I could never grieve,
Whatever misery made me smart.
She sits so firmly in my heart
That by my faith I'd rather not
For all the world think any thought   1110
Without my Lady, I avow.'
    'Sir, by my faith,' I answered, 'now
It seems your luck to be absolved
Before your sins have been resolved.'*
    'Repentance?' challenged he, 'Oh fie!
Repent of loving? Why should I?
For truly then I might as well
Be worse than was Achitophel*
Or foul Antenor – give me joy! –
That traitor who was false to Troy,   1120
Or Ganelon whose faithless breath
Treasonously caused the death
Of Roland and of Oliver.
No, while I live here, I aver,
I'll evermore remember her.'
Then answered I, 'Now, noble sir,
Since you have told me all before,
No need to tell me any more

Just how you saw her first, and where.
Tell me instead the manner fair   1130
And words of your first speech to her.
That is what I long to hear;
And how she first could feel or tell
Whether or not you loved her well.
And tell me too what loss you bore
Which you have talked about before.'
Said he, 'Your words are idle. Yes,
I've lost much more than you can guess.'
'What loss?' I asked. 'You mean that she
Won't have you back? How can that be?   1140
Or have you done some deed amiss,
Which made her leave you? Is it this?
For love of God, please tell me all.'
     'Before God,' answered he, 'I shall.
I say again as I have said;
On her my love was wholly laid.
And that it was, she could not tell
For some long time, believe it well!
For be assured I just dared not
For all this world reveal my thought,   1150
Nor did I wish to rouse her ire.
And why? She was the queen entire
Of all my body; had the heart,
And so from her I could not part.
To keep myself from idleness
I keenly with industriousness
Composed as best I could in song,
And often sang out loud and strong.
Thus very many songs I wrought,
Although my music still fell short,   1160
And so my songs were not well done
Like those of Jubal,* Lamech's son,
Who first found out the art of song;
For as his brother's hammers rung
Upon his anvil up and down,
He took from them the primal sound.

Yet Greeks say that Pythagoras
First found the art of song. It was
Aurora who wrote to that effect* –
No matter which tale is correct!   1170
Anyway, songs I came to write
In passion, for my heart's delight.
Behold! Here is the very first –
I don't know if it was the worst.

   Lord, how that sweet one makes me light
   In heart with thoughts of her delight,
   Who is so beautiful to see!
   I wish to God it might so be
   That she would take me as her knight,
   My Lady, she so fair and bright!   1180

Now have I told you, truth to say,
The first song that I wrote. One day
I thought about the grief and woe
Which for her sake I suffered so,
Although indeed she knew it not,
Nor dared I tell her what I thought.
"Alas!" I sighed, "No remedy!
To tell her would be death to me,
For then I'd dread the consequence:
That she might sharply take offence.   1190
Alas! How then should I proceed?"
   'Thus reasoning, I was sad indeed;
I thought my heart would break in two!
But finally, as I speak true,
I settled in the thought that Nature
Would not produce in one sole creature
So much of beauty and of good,
But yet compassion would exclude.
In hope of that, I told my plight
In pain, though sure it was not right.   1200
I knew, whatever I might try,
I had to tell her, or to die.
So I began, I know not how:

I tell it over badly now.
Besides, God knows, I'm bound to say
It fell on such a luckless day
As brought the plagues to old Egypt;
For many a word I overskipped
In telling her my tale, in terror
Of making a *faux pas* or error.   1210
With grieving heart and wounds which bled,
Quietly, quaking in my dread
And shame, and halting in my tale
In panic, with my face all pale,
By turns going white, then flushing red,
Bowing to her I hung my head.
Her I dared not look upon,
My manners, wit and poise all gone.
I cried out, "Mercy!" and no more.
It was no game. I suffered sore.   1220
    'Eventually, I tell you, when
My fainting heart came back again,
This briefly following was my speech:
Heart-whole, I started to beseech
That she would be my lady sweet.
I swore to her with heartfelt heat
My steadfast duty firm and true,
And love that would be always new.
To guard her honour evermore,
And serve no other, then I swore   1230
To do my best. I promised this:
"For yours is all that ever there is,
My sweetheart. Barring dreams untrue,
I never shall be false to you,
As sure as God's intents prevail!"
    'And when I thus had told my tale,
God knows, my love in pain and awe
She seemed to think not worth a straw.
To tell it briefly as it is,
Her answer was most truly this: 1240
I cannot perfectly convey

54

Exactly what she had to say;
The gist of it was simply "No"
And nothing more. Alas! What woe
That day I knew! I was so rent
With sorrow that the sad lament
Cassandra* made for Ilium
And Troy destroyed could never sum
The extent of what I then went through.
I could not add a word thereto   1250
For utter fear, but stole away.
And thus I lived for many a day,
Nor was there any time of woe
On which I felt the need to go
Beyond my bed's head seeking sorrow;
I found it there on every morrow,
My love for her being no caprice.
   Years passed in all these agonies,
And then there came by luck to hand
My chance to make her understand   1260
My pain; and she well understood
My wish for her was only good:
To honour her and guard her name,
And dread lest she should come to shame,
And serve her keenly. That being so,
'Twere pity I should die in woe,
Seeing I had no foul design.
So when she heard this tale of mine,
My Lady nobly gave to me
Out of her magnanimity   1270
Her mercy, saving honour perforce –
There could not be another course.
To seal the gift she gave a ring,
To me the utmost precious thing.
At that, with joy my heart grew great:
No need to put it to debate!
By God, I was revived as fast
As one from death to life upcast –
Of all events by far the best,

Most joyous and yet most at rest.   1280
In truth that bringer of delight,
When I was wrong and she was right,
Always in generosity
Forgave me most becomingly.
In every youthful circumstance
She took me in her governance.
Always her counsel was so true,
Our joy was ever fresh and new.
Our hearts were so in harmony
That neither was ever contrary   1290
To the other heart when sorrows came.
In truth they bore all things the same
Whatever joy or grief they had.
Alike they were both glad or sad;
Assured in union we were.
And thus we lived for many a year,
So well, I cannot tell you how.'
    'Sir,' asked I, 'where is she now?'
'Now?' echoed he. That stopped him dead.
Then lifeless as a stone, he said,   1300
'Alas the day that I was born!
I told you that I was forlorn
Because of loss that hurt me sore.
Remember what I said before:
I said, "Your words are idle. Yes,
I've lost much more than you can guess."
God knows, alas! that loss was she!'
'Alas, good sir! How can that be?'
'She's dead!' 'O no!' 'She's dead, I swear!'
'Is that your loss? What woe to bear!'   1310
And with that word they stopped as one
And blew the return, for all was done
That day in hunting of the hart.
With that this king made to depart
Upon his homeward way and ride
To a building which was there beside
(The distance from us was but slight):

56

A Long Castle walled in white,*
And by Saint John! on a Rich Mount.
It was as in my dream's account.   1320
And in my dream, as now I tell,
Within that castle was a bell
Which seemed to strike the hour of twelve.
And therewith I awoke myself
And found that I was lying in bed,
And that old book in which I'd read
Of Alcyone and Ceyx the King
And of the gods of slumbering
Was in my hand still firmly caught.
'This is so strange a dream,' I thought,   1330
'That I shall in the course of time
Attempt to put it all in rhyme
As best I can, and that right soon.'
This was my dream; now it is done.

The House of Fame

INTRODUCTION TO
'THE HOUSE OF FAME'

The poem was probably composed in about 1379 and, although speculation exists concerning the possible occasion for its writing, none seems to me worth recording. With the fantastic subject matter, exuberance of composition and wild admixture of the heroic and the downright funny of this poem in mind, it seems Gradgrindish to introduce it initially with reference to its sources. Briefly, then: the poem is regarded as transitional between Chaucer's 'French' and 'Italian' periods. Dante provides the source for several important elements in the poem, but the schema follows the general prescription for the French love vision. The ascent to the House of Fame echoes the ascent to Purgatory; the invocation to Apollo in the Proem to Book Three closely follows a Dantean invocation by which Chaucer was doubtless inspired to claim a lofty role for poetry; the Eagle, together with his science, is also drawn from Dante, but comically metamorphosed; and so on. Ovid and Virgil remain constant sources for classical detail. Other sources – and there are many – are traced in Robinson's Notes, but the poem is very much Chaucer's own.

Although 'The House of Fame' is set out in three 'Books', it is best to look upon its amazing semi-autobiographical poetical process as falling naturally into five sections:

1. Invocation: the Temple of Venus and summary of the *Aeneid*, with the appearance of the Eagle (Book One).
2. Space journey in the Eagle's talons, with in-flight natural science lecture, towards the House of Fame (Book Two).
3. Ascent to, and description of, the House of Fame and its inhabitants (ll. 1091–1519).
4. The judgements of Fame (variously called a Lady, a Queen

61

and a Goddess) on different applicants for fame (ll. 1520–1868).

5. To the Hall of Rumour, where truth and lies fight together to escape (ll. 1869–2158).

The transitions from each part to the next are managed with the skill of a practised narrative poet. The conclusions of Books One and Two markedly achieve the kind of suspense aimed at by good serial writers: at the end of Book One the Eagle appears in downward flight, but begins his positive engagement in the poem only at the beginning of Book Two, and at the end of Book Two, the Eagle deposits the poet amid the 'huge uproar' of the House of Fame, which is not described until the beginning of Book Three. The transitions at lines 1520 and 1869 are abrupt surprises, sprung on the reader when he or she has somehow been made to feel that the previous subject is just about exhausted.

A distinguishing feature of the poem is the easy but always surprising alternation between the heroic and the comic, and the fruitful fusion of the two at need, with subtle satiric effect. Chaucer views everything from the standpoint of the narrator, who on the one hand seems an earnest, guileless and even obtuse inquirer, and on the other really knows what is going on and interprets it in an original way. At the outset the confusing attempt to define different sorts of dream and, in the following Invocation, the comic cùrse on those who misinterpret the dream the poet is about to relate, set the ambiguous tone. Then the double joke at the start of the dream itself – the reference to the longest night of the year and the appalling effort imposed on a pilgrim by a two-mile walk to a shrine – is followed by a condensed re-telling of the *Aeneid*, with emphasis upon Dido, who for the Middle Ages was the major heroic figure of that epic.

The Eagle's domination of Book Two must be enjoyed as a comic *tour de force*, in which the key structural matters of the poem are clearly stated. The message the Eagle brings the poet from Jove is that, although Chaucer in his writings has served Love as best he could, he has done it so far by reference only to books; Jove has the power to give him real illumination on the subject by sending him, with the Eagle's help, to the House of Fame. That real illumination we never receive; Caxton's twelve-line repair to the conclusion when he printed the poem in 1483 (see Notes) ambiguously assumes a positive ending, but modern critics, although many agree in finding the poem loose in construction and uncertain in ending, see Chaucer's point in leaving us with the unresolved juxtaposition of the House of Fame and the Hall of Rumour. I like J. A. W. Bennett's clarifying hallucination (*Chaucer's Book of Fame*, p.122): 'The Palace proper is a royal broadcasting station, the adjacent, but sub-ordinate, house of twigs a kind of office for miscellaneous business.'

If we accept that the final message of the poem concerns the nature of Fame, determined as it is by humankind's not neces-sarily logical or moral reactions to the vicissitudes of Fortune, and that its application is general and not limited to Love, we may be satisfied. But we shall hardly fail to hurrah either the Eagle's farcical self-admiration and his dread that his lecture on the properties of sound may be under-prized, or the poet's ability, even while dizzy with whizzing through space in those talons, to refuse a further lecture, this time on astronomy. In the next verbal collision in the poem – Lady Fame's successive confrontations in her court with applicants for her blessing – the rhetoric is diluted by the force of colloquial speech, and we have the august lady dispensing eternal justice and injustice in the language of popular *fabliau* which we shall meet again when the common sorts of bird offer their opinions on the wooing eagles in 'The Parliament of Birds'.

THE HOUSE OF FAME*

BOOK ONE

May God turn all our dreams to good!
For it's a marvel, by the Rood,
Which gives me musings infinite,
What causes dreams by day or night;
And why fulfilment follows some,
But from others does not come;
Why one's a vision, a phantasy,
And one reveals a prophecy,
One to delude, one to foretell,
Doing this man ill and that man well.   10
Phantasy or oracle, I
Can never tell the reason why.
Let him who better knows the cause
Explain it, for my own mind draws
No sense from it. It is not fit
On such affairs to tire my wit;
On different meanings signified,
What gaps in time the dreams divide,
What causes them, why men surmise
This reason more than that applies;   20
As if dreams were the consequence
Of people's special temperaments.
Or maybe, as some people guess,
They come from brainsick feebleness,
Or self-denial or illness, or
Prison or brothel, sorrows sore;
Or else their normal way of life
Is upset by some inner strife,

As when a man's obsessed by books,
Or melancholy dogs his looks,   30
Or doubt and fear so plague his mind
That no one can a remedy find;
Or else, in some, that contemplation,
Or even holy meditation,
Causes such dreams as often as not;
Or that the hard and cruel lot
Of lovers whose passions make them fret,
With too much doubt or hope beset,
Brings on through their emotion's course
Dreams of visionary force;   40
Or else the spirits with their might
Make men and women dream at night;
Or does the soul, by Nature's way
Being perfect, as men tend to say,
And able to see events to come,
Accordingly warn everyone,
By vision or by phantasy,
What their fortune next will be,
Unlike the flesh that lacks the might
To understand these things aright   50
Because they too obscurely show?
Why such things be, I do not know.
May scholars of this and other themes
Discover all the truth of dreams!
But I shall not in any way
Declare my mind except to say
This prayer: May the Holy Rood
Turn every dream we have to good!
For never since my life began,
Nor in the life of other man,   60
Was dream so marvellous and fair
As that I dreamed, I do declare,
Upon the tenth day of December;*
And everything that I remember
Of it I shall report to you.*

Love Visions

Invocation*

Before I start, so trust me true,
I'll offer up an invocation
With especial veneration
Most promptly to the god of sleep,
Whose rocky cavern is his keep   70
Above the flow of Lethe's stream,*
A hell-flood foul in the extreme,
Beside which the Cimmerians* dwell.
There sleeps this gloomy god of hell
With all his thousand sleepy sons,
By custom ever-sleeping ones.
And to this god of whom I tell
I pray he'll make me prosper well
When I recount my dream aright –
If dreams are subject to his might!   80
May he who moves and governs all
That is and was and ever shall
Be, give delight to those who hear,
In all the dreams they have this year!
And may they also stand in grace
With those they love, and have the place
They wish to be in! May they be
Secure from shame and poverty,
And from bad luck and grief and pain!
Whatever pleases, let them gain,   90
And take it well and scorn it not,
Nor wrongly rate it in their thought
Through being malicious in intent!
But if, presumptuously bent
Through hate or scorn or jealousy,
Contempt or tricks or villainy,
To rate it wrong, I pray to God
That, dream he barefoot, dream he shod,
Every misfortune any man
Has suffered since the world began   100
Shall come to him before he dies.

May he deserve it in such wise
As Croesus,* famous Lydian king,
High on a gibbet hung to swing.
That was how he met his end;
His vision he did not comprehend.
That's the prayer he has from me;
I am no better in charity!
I bade you listen when I spoke:
Hear what I dreamed before I woke.   110

The Dream

On December's tenth day I
At night to slumber went to lie
Exactly where I always lay
To sleep, and went off straight away,
Like one whose walk had worn him out
On two miles' pilgrimage devout
To Holy Leonard's* body tomb,
Whose power would lighten all his gloom.
But as I slept, I dreamt I was
Inside a temple built of glass,   120
In which more statues made of gold
Stood on bases manifold,
More splendidly emblazoned shrines
With pinnacles in jewelled designs,
More portraits fine to a degree,
More images carved artfully
In antique style, than ever I saw.
But where I was, it is most sure
I knew not, but I was aware
That it belonged to Venus* there,   130
That temple; for immediately
In portraiture I saw where she
Was floating naked in the sea.
And she was crowned, as I could see,
With a rose garland white and red,
And with a comb to comb her head.

I saw her doves there, how they flew;
I saw her blind son Cupid* too,
And Vulcan* with his face all brown.
    But as I wandered up and down   140
I found that on a wall there was
Upon a tablet made of brass
Inscribed the following: 'If I can,
I now shall sing arms and the man.
The destined knight of mighty fame
Who fugitive from Troy first came
Much suffering to Italian land,
And trod Lavinium's* river-strand.'
And then at once the tale began
As I shall tell you, every man.   150
    First I saw Troy's ruinous fall.
Sinon the Greek* achieved it all
By putting on a lying face
And telling falsehoods vile and base,
Which got the horse let in to Troy,
And lost the Trojans all their joy.
And next was shown there how the fort
Of Ilium* under attack was brought,
And taken, and King Priam killed
With Polites his son, both stilled   160
By Pyrrhus in his savage spleen.
I saw how Venus, love's own queen,
Seeing the citadel aflame,
Down from the heavens swiftly came
And told her son Aeneas to flee;
And how he fled, and so got free,
Taking, in spite of all the throng,
Anchises* his old father along,
Bearing him on his back away,
Crying 'Alas! and woe the day!'   170
And old Anchises in his hand
Bore the gods of their native land
Which in the burning were not lost.
    And next I saw in all that host

Creusa, Lord Aeneas's wife,
Whom he loved as much as life,
With their little son Iulus,*
And also with Ascanius,
Fleeing and crying out their dread;
'Twas sad to hear them as they fled.   180
Then running through a forest, they
Turned off. Creusa missed the way,
And thus, alas! was lost, but how
She died I can't pretend to know.
I saw him search, and how her ghost
Told him to flee the Greekish host,
And said he must in Italy
Without fail find his destiny.
And when her spirit there appeared,
I felt great pity when I heard   190
Her beg Aeneas in her despair
To guard their little son with care.
There carved, I also saw how he,
His father and his company,
Took ship, set sail and left the strand
For Italy, his promised land,
By the straightest route that they could draw.
You, cruel Juno, there I saw,
The Lord of Heaven Jupiter's wife,
Who have detested all your life   200
The blood of Troy, with maddened eye
Run forth distracted and then cry
On Aeolus, the god of wind,*
To blow a gale of every kind,
Strongly enough to drown and drench
Lord and lady, groom and wench;
Yes, drown the whole Trojan nation,
And none of them to have salvation.
    I saw there such a tempest wake
That every heart would shudder and shake   210
To see it painted on the wall.
    And there I saw, amongst it all,

You Venus, painted, lady dear,
Weeping with grief and many a tear,
Praying to Jupiter on high
To let that fleet in safety lie,
And save Aeneas, Prince of Troy,
Since he was her darling boy.
    I saw Jove kiss her; then he swore
To Venus he would still the uproar.   220
I watched the tempest come to rest
And saw Aeneas, much distressed,
Sail on until he left the sea
And came to Carthage secretly.
I saw Aeneas next day set
Forth with Achates,* and they met
The goddess Venus on the way,
Superbly garbed in the array
In which a noble huntress dresses,
With breezes blowing in her tresses.   230
When he'd seen through her disguise,
Aeneas expressed his grief with sighs,
Lamenting that his ships so fair
Were sunk or lost, he knew not where.
Then Venus solaced him with pity,
And sent him into Carthage city,*
Where she said that he would find
The company he'd left behind.
    To give this matter little space,
She caused Aeneas to win such grace   240
With Dido, who was there the Queen,
That quickly she with ardour keen
Became his love and let him do
All that is to marriage due.
Why should I strain my speaking skill?
Or paint in words by force of will
Such talk of love? That cannot be:
I lack that special faculty.
Besides, to say exactly how
They came to close acquaintance now   250

Would take too long for me to tell,
Too long for you to listen as well.
   I saw Aeneas painted there,
Telling Dido all the care
And woes he suffered while at sea.
   And then was painted there how she
Created him with just one word
Her life, her love, her joy, her lord,
And did him every reverence,
Lavishing on him all expense   260
That any woman might perform,
Considering all was in due form,
As he declared; she thereby deemed
That he was virtuous, as he seemed.
Alas! What harm face values do
When in essence they're untrue!
For he to her a traitor was,
And hence she killed herself, alas!
How woman is in error, lo!
To love a man she does not know!   270
By Christ, it's often thus: Behold!
All that glitters is not gold.
For may I keep my head intact,
But under godly looks in fact
May be concealed a wicked vice.
So let no one of taste precise
Take on a lover for looks alone,
Or speech, or manner, or friendly tone.
For every woman may discover
The essential nature of her lover,   280
Which makes him seem what all admire
Until he gets his whole desire;
And then some reason he will find
To swear that she has been unkind,
Furtive, untrue or underhand.
I say all this of Aeneas and
Queen Dido with her foolish lust,
Who too soon loved a guest on trust.

Therefore I quote this true proverb:
'He who really knows a herb   290
May safely apply it to his eye.'
That saying for certain is no lie.
    But let us of Acneas tell
How to treachery he fell,
Deserting Dido brutally.
So when she knew decisively
That he would leave her faithlessly
And go from her to Italy,
She wrung her hands and cried, 'Alas!
What woe for me is come to pass!   300
Alas! Is every man so true?
Each year to have a lover new?
Or if his love so long endure,
Why not three at once, for sure?
Like this: from one he'd get the fame
Of having magnified his name.
The next for friendship he'd agree,
And then of course the third would be
For his delight and sensual bliss;
Lo! All the profit would be his.'   310
With words like this, in her great pain,
Dido loudly did complain,
As I truly dreamed that night:
No other author do I cite.
'Alas, my darling heart!' said she,
'Take pity on my misery!
Don't kill me now! Don't go away!
O wretched Dido, woe the day!'
So cried she to herself anew.
'O Aeneas, what will you do?   320
O that your love, and not the troth
You plighted me with hand and oath,
Nor yet my cruel death,' said she,
'Might hold you still to stay with me!
O look upon my death with rue!
For certainly, my dear heart, you

Know very well that never yet
Did I by any use of wit
Do wrong to you in deed or thought.
O is the speech of men so wrought   330
With seeming virtue but no truth?
Alas, that woman should show ruth
At any time to any man!
I know it now, and well I can
See wretched women lack all art.
For certainly the greater part
Shall similarly be served each one.
However much you men may moan,
As soon as you have won our heart,
You show us your deceiving art.   340
For though your love may seem to last
A season, wait till that is past,
And then see what occurs to you,
What in the end you mean to do.
   'Ah woe the day that I was born!
Through you my name is lost and gone,
And all my acts are read and sung
Throughout the land by every tongue.
O wicked Fame! There cannot be
A thing that moves as swift as she!   350
Yes, all is known and nothing missed,
Though it be covered with a mist.
Indeed, though I might live for ever,
Undo what I have done I never
Shall be able to. My name
Through Aeneas is brought to shame.
This judgement shall be made of me:
"Having done it once, now she
Will do it again most certainly."
So say the people furtively.'   360
But what is done can't be undone:
Her cries and moans so woebegone
For sure availed her not a straw.
   And when she knew and really saw

73

That he'd embarked with all his fleet,
Into her room she made retreat,
And called upon her sister Anne,
And her lament to her began,
Saying the blame was due to her
Because she counselled her to err   370
By taking Aeneas as her lover.
But what! Those words and actions over,
She stabbed herself right through the heart;
The pain tore life and her apart.
But of the way in which she died,
And of the words she dying sighed,
If you further wish to read,
See Virgil in the *Aeneid*,*
Or the *Epistle* of Ovid,*
For what she wrote and how she died;   380
And were it not too long to write,
By God! I'd pen it here all right.

   The harm, the pity, alas the day,
That come when men in love betray!
Such things in books you often read,
And see them daily too in deed.
To think of them brings sadness on.
The Duke of Athens, Demophon,*
Forswore himself most treacherously,
Betraying Phyllis wickedly,   390
The daughter of the King of Thrace,
By dodging wedding date and place;
And when she found he was untrue,
She hanged herself – what else to do? –
Because he had been false and bad.
Does not such anguish make you sad?

   Think how treacherous and remiss
Achilles was to Briseis,*
And Paris was to Oenone,
And Jason to Hypsipyle,   400
And Jason again to Medea;
And Hercules to Deianira,

For he left her for Iole,
Which brought about his death, you see.
How treacherous was Theseus too,
Who, as appears in story true,
Left Ariadne to console
Her sister, devil rot his soul!
For laugh he, frown he, he'd been dead,
The Minotaur had on him fed   410
Had Ariadne not been there.
Because she gave him loving care,
From death contriving his escape,
He played her a disloyal jape.
Being saved, within a little while
He left her sleeping on an isle,
A desolate sea-girt place unknown,
And stealing off, left her alone:
And with her sister Phaedra he
Boarded his ship and went to sea.   420
And yet he'd sworn an oath to her
By all by which a man might swear
That he would have her as his wife
Provided she would save his life:
For she desired nothing else.
It's true: that's what the story tells.
    To mitigate Aeneas's case
A little in his great disgrace,
The book* recounts that Mercury
Told him to go to Italy,   430
Deserting Africa as well
As Dido with her citadel.
    There I saw painted how Aeneas
On course for Italy, met a fierce
Tempest in which his steersman
Was lost soon after it began
Through carelessness; the tiller swept
Him overboard even while he slept.
    Besides all that, I saw as well
Near an isle, going down to hell,   440

75

Aeneas and the Sybil,* to find
Anchises of the lordly mind.
Palinurus* he found thus,
And Dido, and Deiphobus;*
He saw all torments known to hell,
And they would take too long to tell.
Whoever wants to know should read
The many lines about the deed
In Virgil, Dante, Claudian,*
Who cover well the story's span.   450
I saw Aeneas come to land
Safe on the Italian strand,
His treaty with Latinus, King
Of Latium, and his soldiering
In battle, fighting with his knights,
Before establishing his rights.
I saw him take King Turnus'* life
And win Lavinia for his wife,
And all the marvellous signs there were
From heavenly gods in this affair,   460
And how in spite of what was done
By Juno's tricks, Aeneas won,
Achieving all he wished to do
Because high Jove had seen him through
At Venus's request and boon.
May all of us be saved as soon,
And may she make our sorrows light!
    When I'd seen all this splendid sight
In that noble temple thus,
I thought, 'Ah Lord that madest us,   470
I never saw such excellence
In images, such opulence,
As in that church I saw on show.
But still who made them I don't know,
Nor do I know where I could be.
But now I shall go out and see
At the wicket-gate, if I can
Find anywhere a stirring man

Who can tell me where I am.'
When I out of the wicket came,   480
I looked around and all my eyes
Saw was a field of massive size,
Stretching as far as eye could see,
Without a town, or house, or tree,
Or bush, or grass, or ploughing land;
In all that field was only sand
Composed of many tiny grains,
As on Libya's desert plains;
Nor could I see a single creature
Of a kind produced by Nature   490
To give me help of any sort.
'O Christ who art in bliss!' I thought,
'From false dream and from phantasy
Preserve me!' And in piety
Up to the heavens my eyes I cast.
Then I became aware at last
That right beside the sun, as high
As I could pierce with my eye,
I seemed to see an eagle soar
Larger by far than heretofore   500
I'd seen in birds of eagle breed.
But true as death, in very deed,
This bird was shining golden bright:
You'd never see so fine a sight,
Unless the heavens should gain and hold
Another glorious sun of gold.
So shone the eagle's feathers bright
As downward then it dipped its flight.

BOOK TWO

Proem

Now men of all sorts, old and young,
Who understand the English tongue,   510
Hear this my dream for the first time,
And learn from it a lesson sublime.
Such dream it was, as visions go,

Love Visions

That not Isaiah nor Scipio,
Not Nebuchadnezzar, king of yore,
Not Pharaoh, Turnus, Helcanor,*
Ever dreamed a dream like this.
Now, blissful, beautiful Cypris,*
Grant me your favour at this time!
And help me to compose in rhyme,   520
You gods that on Parnassus dwell,
By Helicon, the crystal well!*
O Thought, that shaped my phantasy
And shut it in the treasury
That is my brain, now men shall see
If you possess the quality
And force to tell my dream aright:
So now make known your skill and might!

The Dream

That eagle, whose approach I told,
Shining with feathers as of gold,   530
And apt at such a height to soar,
I came to gaze on more and more,
To see its beauty and its wonder;
But never did a crash of thunder
Or lightning bolt which with its power
Smashed to dust a mighty tower,
Descending swiftly all aflame,
Come down so fast as this bird came,
When he perceived me roaming free
In that waste locality.   540
And in his claws so grim and strong
Tipped with talons sharp and long
He seized me, swooping as I fled,
Then soared again with wings outspread,
Carrying me in those talons stark
With ease, as if I were a lark,
So high, I cannot tell how high
Or by what means; I knew not, I.

For every faculty I possessed
Was stunned, bewildered and oppressed: 550
What with his soarings and my dread
My senses went all blank and dead
Because my terror was so strong.
   So in his claws I lay for long,
Till at the last to me he spake
In human voice and said, 'Awake!
Don't be so terrified, for shame!'
And then he called me by my name;
Indeed I thought he said, 'Awake!'
The better my deep trance to break   560
Exactly in the voice and tone
Of one whose name to me was known.
And when I heard that voice so plain,
My mind came back to me again,
For it was kindlier said to me
Than ever it was wont to be.
   So coming to at that, I stirred,
Held in the claws of that great bird,
Who then knew I had living heat,
And also that my heart did beat.   570
He started having fun with me,
And spoke to me consolingly,
Twice exclaiming, 'Holy Mary!
What a trial you are to carry!
As if there could be any need!
For sure as God helps me in deed,
No harm shall come to you from this.
The reason for your airing is
That you shall learn and gain from it.
What! Dare you look about you yet?   580
Be brave and know assuredly
I am your friend.' And therewith I
Began to wonder. 'God,' I thought,
'Who made all beings of every sort!
Is there no other way to die?
Is Jove about to stellify

My soul? What else is in his mind?
I'm not Elijah or Enoch's kind,
Or Romulus or Ganymede,*
Who was caught up, as you may read,   590
To heaven by Lord Jupiter
And made the high gods' cup-bearer.'
Behold, this was my phantasy,
But he who carried me could see
What I was thinking, and said thus:
'Your judgement is erroneous,
For Jove is not the least inclined –
So put it firmly out of mind –
To turn you yet into a star.
I shall not bear you very far   600
Before I tell you what I am,
Where you are going, and why I came
To do this job, so kindly take
Good heart, and don't in terror quake.'
'Gladly,' said I. And he said, 'Know
First, I whose talons hold you so,
Which makes you shake with fear and wonder,
Am dwelling with the God of Thunder,
Whom men on earth call Jupiter,
Who often sends me flying far   610
To carry out his high intent.
And that is why I have been sent
To you; so listen, on your oath!
Sure, pity and compassion both
He has for you because so long
You've keenly served with ardour strong
Blind Cupid, his adored nephew,
And Cupid's mother, Venus, too,
Without reward at all as yet,
In spite of which you've set your wit –   620
Not much of that your head contains –
To writing books and songs, refrains
In rhyme, with rhythmic rise and fall,
As best you could, a faithful thrall

Of Love and of his servants too,
Who sought, and seek, his service true.
You strove to praise his subtle art,
Though you possessed of it no part;
For all which reasons, God bless me,
Jove counts it great humility   630
And virtue too, that you will make
Often at night your head to ache,
Writing in your study of Love,
Composing evermore of Love,
Singing out his honour and praise,
And chronicling his followers' ways,
Their every move and stratagem,
And scorning neither him nor them,
Although you're caught up in the dance
Of those whom Love will not advance.   640
     'And truly that is why I find
That Jupiter has you in mind.
Another cause, sir, yet ensues:
It is that you have brought no news
Of Love's adepts in search of bliss,
Or other things God made as his,
Not only can you nothing learn
From distant lands; the near concerns
Of neighbours at your very door
Are things you simply don't explore.   650
This news and that you always shun,
For when your daily work is done
And you've made all your reckonings,
You do not rest or seek new things,
But off you go back home alone
And sit as dumb as any stone,
Poring over another book
Until your eyes have a glazed look.
You live as hermits do, I say,
Though not abstemiously as they.   660
     'And therefore Jupiter, through his grace,
Wills me to take you to a place

Most fitly styled the House of Fame,
To amuse you there, as in a game,
In recompense for your devotion,
Your travails, and the deep emotion
And pain that you have been put through
By Cupid, who cares not for you!
Thus Jove will through his virtue's sense
Provide you with due recompense,   670
And give your spirit much good cheer.
Believe it, man! For you shall hear
When you and I have landed there,
Most wondrous things, I do declare:
More doings of Love's devotees,
Some true and some false histories;
How many loves are new begun;
How long devoted loves are won;
How some loves accidentally
Crop up, and no one can tell why,   680
Just as a blind man starts a hare;
Much mirth and fuss shall you see there,
As lovers find their love steel-true,
Or so they think, good through and through;
More discords and more jealousies,
More mutterings, more novelties,
More tricks and more dissimulations
And hollow reconciliations;
More scissorless and razorless
Beard trimmings in two hours or less   690
Performed than there are grains of sand;
More false hopes fondly held in hand,
And many desperate patching acts
On long-abandoned loving pacts,
More dispute-settlings, love-accords
Than on instruments are chords;
And more interchange of love
Than grains of corn that barns know of –
Now could you credit it?' said he.
'No, God's wisdom succour me!'   700

I answered. 'Why?' he asked. 'For it
Could scarcely be, so says my wit,
That Fame, although she may command
All chattering magpies in the land,
All spies as well, could hear all this,
Or those spies see it,' I said. 'Oh yes!'
Said he, 'That I can well attest
With reasons you cannot contest,
Provided you with keen intent
Hear and follow my argument.   710
    'Learn first where Fame the goddess dwells:
It's as your favourite author* tells.
Her palace is positioned, I say,
Exactly at a point midway
Between the heavens and earth and sea,
So whatever in all those three
Is said in secret or openly,
The way to it is wholly free
Because it's placed with such great care
That every sound must go straight there;   720
Whatever comes from any tongue,
Be it whispered, read or sung,
Or said in confidence or fear,
Is bound to go there sounding clear.
    'Now listen closely, for I will
With first-class logic posed with skill
Give you a splendid demonstration
Of my profound ratiocination.
    'Geoffrey, I'm sure that you know this:
Every natural thing that is*   730
Has a habitat where it
Can best preserve its essence fit,
To which location every thing,
Its own true nature favouring,
When it's far away from thence,
Strives to go with every sense.
Lo! Any day you'd chance to see
Some heavy object as, e.g.

Big stone, or lead, some thing of weight,
Which when you lift it to a height   740
And let it go, it falls right down.
Just so I say of fire or sound
Or smoke, or other substance light;
Each one strives upward to a height.
While all are free, the light will tend
To rise, the heavy to descend.
And that's the reason why you see
All rivers flowing to the sea;
Their nature tells them so to flow.
Likewise I find that fishes know   750
Their habitat is flood and sea;
And trees in earth are glad to be.
Thus everything, you see by that,
Has its appointed habitat,
To which it always will repair
Because it suffers no harm there.
Behold! Such thinking's always found
In what philosophers expound!
Aristotle, Plato too,
And other writers hold this view: 760
And to confirm what I propound,
You know this well, that speech is sound:
Otherwise it could not be heard.*
So now I'll teach you, mark my word.
    'Sound is only air that's broken.
And every single word that's spoken,
Aloud or secret, foul or fair,
Is in its essence only air;
For just as flame is smoke that's lit,
So sound is air which has been split.   770
But this takes place in many ways,
Two of which I'll put in phrase:
The music of the pipe, and harp.
For when the puff in pipe is sharp,
The air is rent with violence
And split. Behold! I speak pure sense!

And when a harp-string's given a touch,
Whether with little force or much,
Behold! The air breaks with the noise
Just as it does with human voice.   780
And that's the truth concerning speech!
    'And now the next thing I shall teach
Is that every speech, noise, sound,
With amplified effect is found
– Even the squeaking of a mouse –
To come perforce to Fame's own house.
I prove it thus – take good heed now! –
By experiment. For if you throw
A stone into a pool, you know
Quite well the splash it makes will grow   790
Into a ring, a little round
As big as on a pot-lid's found.
And then you see what that will bring;
The ring will cause another ring,
And that a third, and so forth, brother,
Each circle caused making another
Wider than itself; so thence
From small to huge circumference
Each circle makes another ring
And causes that one's broadening,   800
And all expand until at last
The process goes so far and fast
The banks are overflowed all over.
Your eye above might not discover
That because it happens under –
Which you may think a mighty wonder.
And anyone who says I lie,
Then let him prove the contrary!
And truly, just as every word
That's shouted out or hardly heard   810
To start with moves the air about,
And by this moving, without doubt,
At once another air is moved,
As I have by the water proved,

85

With each circle causing another;
Just so of air, beloved brother.
Each air stirs up another one
Increasingly; and once begun
Then voice or noise or word or sound
With amplified effect is bound   820
To travel to the House of Fame.
Take that in earnest or in game!
    'I've told you, if you call to mind,
How speech and sound and all their kind
Upwards by nature strive to move:
This, you perceive, I clearly prove.
And that same place, I dare be sworn,
To which a thing is always drawn,
Has its natural position:
That shows with absolute precision   830
That the natural living ground
Of every speech and every sound,
Whether it be foul or fair,
Is found by nature in the air.
And since each living thing must go
From its location, as all know,
To that position which I say
Is natural, if it's far away,
As I proved to you before,
It follows that each sound, for sure,   840
Proceeds by nature from its base
Towards its natural homing place.
And this same place of which I tell
Where Lady Fame is pleased to dwell
Is equidistant from these three:
The heavens, the earth, and last, the sea,
Because that best preserves the sound.
This conclusion then is found:
That every speech of every man,
From when the very first began,   850
Has risen and gone with perfect aim
By nature to the House of Fame.

'Now have I not, just tell me true,
Proved that simple fact to you
Without recourse to subtlety
Of speech or great prolixity
Of terms drawn from philosophy,
Or ornaments from poetry,
Or rhetorical figures cited?
By God, you ought to be delighted!   860
For complex language and involved
Argument cannot be resolved
Both together: you must confess
That's true!' he ended. I said, 'Yes.'
     'Aha!' he went on, 'Lo! I can
Talk in lay terms to a lay man,
And of such lofty knowledge speak
That he may shake it by the beak
And find it palpable and true!
But tell me now, I beg of you,   870
What did you think of my conclusion?'
'An irrefutable effusion,'
Said I. 'And things are like to be
Exactly as you've proved to me.'
'By God and by my halidom!'
He said, 'You'll have before night come
The proof by clear experiment
Of each word in my argument,
And top and tail and every bit
Your ears shall hear the truth of it: 880
That every single spoken word
Comes to Fame's House and is heard
As I have said. What would you more?'
Upon which words, he rose to soar,
Saying the while, 'By Saint James,
Now we'll have some fun and games.'
     'How do you feel?' he asked of me.
'All right,' I said. 'Now look,' said he,
'Tell me truly, looking down,
Whether you recognize a town   890

87

Or house or other habitation:
If you can make such affirmation,
Be sure to warn me so that I
Can tell you then immediately
How far from it you are up here.'

   I looked down then and saw all clear
Meadow and plain in full detail
And hill and mountain, down and dale,
Valley and wood, conspicuous features,
And just descried some mighty creatures.   900
Now rivers, now great cities and more,
Now towns and mighty trees I saw,
And big ships sailing on the sea.

   But quickly in a flash did he
Fly up above the ground so high
That all the world seemed to my eye
No bigger than a tiny dot.
Or else the air was, like as not,
Too thick for sight to penetrate.
And then he spoke with ardour great: 910
'D'you see a sign of any town
Or place you know of there far down?'
'No.'·'No wonder that!' said he,
'For never half so high as we
Was Alexander of Macedon,*
Or Scipio named African,
Who saw most clearly in a dream
Both hell and earth, and heaven supreme;
Nor even wretched Daedalus,
Nor yet his child, weak Icarus,*   920
Who flew so high the heat of the sun
Melted his wings, and down he spun
To soak in the sea and there be drowned:
Laments for him were quite profound.

   'And now,' said he, 'Turn up your face,
And look upon this mighty space,
This air; and take care not to be
Afraid of what you there shall see;

For in this lofty region dwell
Many beings reported well   930
In Plato's works. So now behold
The Skyey Beasts* so many-fold!'
And so I saw that company,
Both those that walk and those that fly.
He then said, 'Look up still more high,
And there behold the Galaxy,
Which men have named the Milky Way
Because it's white (and faith, I say,
Some even call it Watling Street*),
And which was scorched and burnt with heat   940
When, be advised, the Sun's own son,
Phaeton,* tried to drive alone
And guide his father's chariot.
The horses were not slow to spot
The lad's mishandling at a glance,
And they began to buck and prance,
Throwing him now up, now down,
Until he saw the Scorpion,
A sign that stays in heaven yet.
And he in terror lost his wit   950
At that and dropped the reins and freed
The horses, which with sudden speed
First galloped up, then downwards turned
Until both air and earth were burned;
Then Jupiter killed him on the spot
And threw him from the chariot.
Lo, is it not an error large
To let an idiot have charge
Of something that he can't control?'
And with those words, upon my soul   960
Still higher he began to soar,
And cheered me ever more and more,
He spoke to me so truthfully.
   I looked around and under me
And saw the Skyey Beasts below,
The clouds and mists and storms and snow

And hailstorms, rain and driving winds,
And all creation of right kinds,
Through which I'd travelled. 'God!' said I,
'Creator of Adam nobly high.   970
Great is your power of every kind!'
Then Boethius came into my mind
Who wrote, 'A thought may fly so high
With feathers of philosophy
It passes the celestial sphere,
Transcending earth in its career;
And at its back it sees the clouds –'
Such thoughts I spoke: they came in crowds.
    Then I was seized with doubt and fear
And said, 'I know that I am here,   980
But whether I am flesh or ghost
I know not: God, thou surely know'st!'
For never yet was sent to me
Perception of such clarity.
And then I thought of Marcian,*
And next of Anticlaudian,*
Who both once gave descriptions fair
Of all the heavenly regions there,
At least, as far as then I saw.
I can believe them now therefore.   990
    With that the eagle gave a cry:
'Leave off your dreaming phantasy!
Concerning stars, why not learn that?'
'No fear! Not me!' I answered flat.
'Why not?' 'Because I am too old.'
'If you'd said, "Yes", I would have told,'
He said, 'the names of stars to you,
And all the heavenly signs thereto,
And which they are.' 'No matter,' said I.
'Yes, by God!' said he, 'And why?   1000
Because when you read poetry,
How gods proceed to stellify
Bird, fish or beast, or him or her,
As Raven, Great Bear, Little Bear,*

Arion with his harp so fine,
Castor and Pollux, the Dolphin sign,
Or Atlas's fair daughters seven,
Each one of which is set in heaven,
You often think about them, though
Where they are placed, you just don't know.'   1010
'No matter!' I said, 'There is no need.
I take their word – may I have God-speed! –
Who wrote of things in this high sphere
As if I knew their places here.
Besides, up here they shine so bright
I might be blinded by the light
If I gazed on them.' 'Maybe,'
He said, and went on carrying me
A while, then gave the loudest shout
I'd ever heard, and thus cried out: 1020
'Saint Julian's* helped us to arrive,
So raise your head and look alive!
Behold, the House of Fame is here!
Can you not hear what I can hear?'
'What?' I asked. 'The mighty sound,'
He said, 'that rumbles up and down
The House of Fame conveying tidings
Both of compliments and chidings,
Of lies and truth all mixed, I swear.
So listen! There's no whispering there.   1030
Can't you hear the roaring sough?'
Said I, 'By God, yes, well enough.'
'And what sound is it like?' asked he.
'By Peter, like the crash of sea,'
I said, 'against great hollowing rocks*
When ships are swallowed in tempest shocks;
Or like the din a man would hear
A mile away drum in his ear.
Or like the rumble after the last
Mighty clap of a thunder-blast,   1040
When Jove has struck apart the air.
It makes me sweat with fear, I swear!'

Said he, 'Don't let such things affright you;
There's nothing there that wants to bite you.
You'll come to no harm, honestly.'
   And as he spoke, both he and I
Had neared the place, which there below
Was well within a spear's throw.
I don't know how, but in a street
He set me fairly on my feet,   1050
And said, 'Walk forth a bit: advance
And seek adventure; take what chance
May offer in the House of Fame.'
   I answered, 'If it's all the same,
And while we've time, before I go,
For the love of God please let me know –
In truth I'll give a willing ear –
If this loud din that I can hear
Is made, as I have heard you tell,
By people who on earth do dwell,   1060
And comes here in the very way
You outlined earlier today;
And that there's nobody at all
Before us in this mighty hall,
Making all this huge uproar.'
'No, by Saint Clare!*' the eagle swore,
'And guide me, wisest God above!
But one thing I must warn you of,
A thing that's bound to make you wonder.
Lo! to the House of Fame up yonder   1070
Comes all men's speech, I've made it plain.
No need to teach you that again.
But grasp this further: when a speech
Arrives within that house's reach,
Then straight away it starts to take
The form its speaker used to make*
On earth below when it was said,
Whether clothed in black or red;
And has a likeness so exact
To the speaker that you'd swear in fact   1080

It must the self-same body be,
Man or woman, he or she.
Now, isn't that a marvellous thing?'
'Yes,' said I then, 'by heaven's King!'
These words exchanged, he said, 'Adieu!
I'll stay here and I'll wait for you.
May God in heaven send you grace
To learn some good thing in this place!'
I took my leave without delay
And towards the palace made my way.   1090

BOOK THREE

Invocation

O God of wisdom and of light,
Apollo, through thy glorious might
Favour this little book, the last!
Not that I'd have it highly classed
As poetry, to give delight;
But since the rhymes are crude and light,
Yet make it, please, at least agreeable,
Though verses often lack a syllable;
Because my effort is not seen
In graces, but in what I mean.   1100
And if, Divinest Virtue, thou
Wilt help me to exhibit now
What's clearly printed in my head –
Behold! It should be boldly said:
It's to describe the House of Fame –
Thou'lt see me go with certain aim
To the nearest laurel that I see
And kiss it, for it is thy tree.
Now quickly come into my breast!

The Dream

Leaving the eagle, I addressed   1110
Myself to studying the place.

93

Before my verses further pace,
I shall describe the house and site
In detail and in form, then write
Of how I scaled the rocky height
On which that castle stood in might:
There's not a higher one in Spain.
But up I climbed in utter pain,
And though to climb was hard for me,
Yet keenly I desired to see   1120
By gazing as I bent down low,
If somehow I could come to know
What sort of stone this high rock was.
Crystalline alum in form of glass
It seemed, but that it shone more bright,
Yet what compacted substance might
Compose it was not clear to me.
But I perceived eventually
It was wholly, in essence real,
A rock of ice, and not of steel.   1130
'By Saint Thomas à Becket!' I thought,
'Foundation of a feeble sort
On which to build a house so high!
The builder of it I deny
The right to boast, God save my soul!'
    Then saw I carved along the whole
Of one side famous names galore
Of folk who'd prospered long before,
Whose fame had blown the wide world over.
But scarcely could my eyes recover   1140
The shapes of any letters for me
To read their names; for certainly
They'd thawed and were so lost to view
That of the letters one or two
Had melted out of every name –
And thus *un*famous was their fame!
Men well say: 'What can ever last?'
    I pondered then how they had passed
Away. Did they not melt in heat?

Or founder in the tempest-beat? 1150
For on the other side, I say,
Of that great height which northward lay,
The hill was carved with many a name
Whose owner had enjoyed great fame
In olden times, and yet they were
As fresh as if the writing there
Were done that day, that hour indeed
When I'd arrived to gaze and read.
Of course I knew exactly why
All those words before my eye 1160
Had been preserved: because they stayed
Within a lofty castle's shade.
Besides it was so high a place
That heat was powerless to deface.
Then up the hill I made my way
And found upon its crest, I say,
A building of such loveliness
That no man living could express
Its beauty by his verbal art,
Nor yet design its counterpart, 1170
Then build a perfect copy of it
Which might in beauty rival it,
Being most marvellously wrought.
Yes, every time I give it thought,
That castle astounds me; and my wit,
Striving to tell the truth of it,
The beauty and superb design,
And craft in every detail fine,
Cannot meet such a high demand.
I can't describe it, understand? 1180
    But all the same I hold in mind
The essential things of every kind.
Thus, by Saint Giles,* to me it seemed
That everything in beryl gleamed,
Both the castle and the tower,
The hall and every room and bower –
A jointless whole without a flaw.

But yet much delicate work I saw:
Pinnacles, turrets, ornament,
Niches, gargoyles excellent,   1190
While many windows made a show
Like heavy flakes in a storm of snow.
Carved deep in every turret's face
Were niches, various in their grace,
In which there stood all round about
That castle, always facing out,
Statues of minstrels most diverse
And story-tellers who rehearse
Romances of both joy and grief,
A sphere in which Fame rules as chief.   1200
 Orpheus* I heard harping there
With truest tune and tone most fair –
Musicianship supremely high!
And playing at his side close by
There sat Arion with his lyre,*
Chiron, the centaurs' wisest sire,
The Breton bard Glasgerion,
And other harpists many a one.
And little harpists sat below,
Each with his harp most apropos,   1210
And looking up at them agape
In imitation like an ape:
Art miming Nature, you might say.
 I saw behind, not far away
From these performing by themselves,
At least a thousand men times twelve
Playing music of various forms
On bagpipes, oboes, strident shawms
And many more wind instruments.
Their playing was all excellence   1220
On dulcet and reed-pipe, which grace
The ox-roast at the feasting-place,
And trumpet, flute and lilting horn,
And rough pipes fashioned from green corn,
Music of shepherd-boy or groom

Who guards his livestock in the broom.
I saw Athenian Pseustis there,*
Atiteris and, I declare,
The satyr Marsyas, whose skin
Was flayed from body, face and chin   1230
Because he claimed to pipe as well
As God Apollo, sages tell.
I saw famed pipers old and young,
Speakers of Teutonic tongue,
Teaching love- and leaping-dances,
Rounds and other steps and fancies.
Then saw I in another place
Standing in an open space
Those who blow the clarion sounds
Of bugle and trump on battle-grounds,   1240
For stirring clarion calls are right
Where blood is shed in deadly fight.
I heard Misenus, trumpeter famed,*
Whom Virgil in the *Aeneid* named.
I listened there while Joab blew,
Thiodamas and others too;
And all who blew the clarion
In Catalonia and Aragon
And were illustrious in their day
For trumpeting, I there heard play.   1250
Sitting nearby, a host immense
Were playing different instruments
Whose names I know not, numberless
As stars are in the sky, I guess;
And these I shall not put in rhyme
To spoil your ease or waste your time.
For time that's gone you can't retrieve
By any means, you must believe.
Minstrels, magicians, conjurors
I saw performing, sorcerers,   1260
Charm-spellers too and sorceresses,
Ancient witches, Pythonesses
Who work in smoky emanations

At exorcisms and incantations;
And scholars too who know the arts
Of natural magic in their hearts,
At some ascendants with their skill
Making images which will
Through magic of the Zodiac
Cure the sick or set them back.   1270
Queen Medea I there did view,*
And Circe and Calypso too;
There saw I Hermes Belinous,
Simon Magus and Elymas.
I saw them there, knew them by name:
By such art great men have their fame.
Colle the magician there I saw
Upon a table of sycamore
Perform a trick most strange to tell:
I saw him put a whole windmill   1280
Under a tiny walnut-shell.
    Why should I draw it out and tell
From now until the Day of Doom
Exactly what I saw and whom?
When I had marked those people well
And found myself still free, I fell
To musing and considered long
Those beryl walls so fine and strong,
Which shone more luminous than glass
And made each thing seem to surpass   1290
Itself in worth and in acclaim –
That is the natural way with Fame!
I wandered forth till I came straight
On my right hand to the castle gate,
Whose carving was so fine that none
So beautiful was ever done;
And yet what made that building fair
Derived from chance as much as care.
No need to make you longer dwell
Upon this portal while I tell   1300
Its images, embellishments,

Ingenious carvings, ornaments
And hacked out masonry such as
The corbel and its figured mass.
But Lord! How lovely to behold!
For all was leafed in carven gold.
So in I went, no pause for doubt,
And met a crowd there crying out:
'Largess! A bounty! Do us grace!
God save the lady of this place,   1310
Our own true noble Lady Fame,
And those who wish to win their name
From us!' I heard that cry from all.
Quickly they came then from the hall,
Jingling coins both silver and gold;
And some were kings-at-arms with bold
Shapes of diamond on their crowns,
And ribbons on their splendid gowns,
And many fringes on them too.

   I saw that those who came in view   1320
Were heralds and pursuivants all,
Who praised rich people with their call.
And every single officer there,
As I most truly can declare,
Had on a garment which men call
A coat of arms. Yes, one and all
Wore rich-embroidered surcoats* there;
Though all were different, all were fair.
But now I shall not, as I live
All the lively detail give   1330
Of all the escutcheons that I saw
Upon those surcoats that they wore.
The task would be impossible,
For all the detail told in full
Would make a twenty-foot-thick book!
If one who knew them undertook
To scan the arms, he'd see all those
Of famous men that Europe knows,
And Africa and Asia too,

99

From when the knightly code first grew.   1340
Lo! How can I convey all this?
About the great hall, what need is
To say to you that every wall
Of it, and floor and roof and all,
Was half a foot thick golden plate,
And none was in a shabby state,
But proved as fine in every way
As ducat from Venice any day,
Of which my purse contains too few?
Each surface was set thickly through   1350
With foils containing jewels as fair
As those the Lapidary* calls rare,
Profuse as grass in any dell.
But it would take too long to tell
Their names, so I'll proceed apace.
   Within this fine luxurious place
So pleasant called the House of Fame,
No mighty press of people came,
Nor was there overcrowding there.
But on a dais high and fair,   1360
Seated on an imperial throne
Entirely made of ruby stone –
A carbuncle that jewel is called –
I saw in permanence installed
In state a splendid female creature,
So beautifully formed by Nature
There could not be a lovelier.
And first of all, as I aver,
She was, I thought, so small and slight
That no more than a cubit's height   1370
In very truth she seemed to be;
Yet being thus, she suddenly,
Miraculously, grew and so,
With feet upon the earth below,
Yet with her head reached up to heaven,
Where there shine the planets seven.
And in my judgement a still more

Extraordinary thing I saw
When I looked upon her eyes;
I could not count them anywise.   1380
She had as many, take my word,
As there are feathers on a bird,
Or on the feathered creatures four*
Who to God's throne such honour bore
In the Apocalypse, John's book.
Curling and wavy, her hair shook
Like burnished gold reflecting light,
And she besides – I truly write –
Had as many upstanding ears
And tongues as on a beast are hairs;   1390
And swiftly growing on her feet
I saw wings of the partridge fleet.
    But Lord! The jewels, wealth limitless
I saw adorning this goddess!
And Lord! The heavenly melody
Of songs most full of harmony
As round her throne I heard the singing
That set the palace walls all ringing!
There sang the Muse of Epic, she
Whom all men call Calliope;*   1400
And her eight sisters too were there
Whose faces seemed most meekly fair,
And evermore continually
They sang of Fame, as there heard I:
'All praise to thee and to thy name,
Thou goddess of Renown and Fame!'
    Then I perceived there finally,
When I chanced to look up high,
That this noble queen upon
Her shoulders wore inscribed and drawn   1410
The coat of arms and the true name
Of every soul that won great fame:
Alexander, Hercules –
A shirt concluded his life's lease!*
Thus seated saw I this goddess

In honour, wealth and worthiness,
Concerning whom I'll cease to prate
While other matters I relate.
I saw there standing on each side,
And leading to the portals wide   1420
Down from the dais, columns made
Of metal which no gleams displayed.
But though their value was not great,
Yet they were made for high estate,
And people worthy of reverence
And noble and lofty sentiments
Were on the columns standing high.
To tell you of them now I'll try.
   First of all then I saw there
Upon a column tall and fair   1430
All made of lead and iron fine
Him of the sect called saturnine,*
Josephus,* that great jew of old,
Who all the Hebrew history told,
And on his shoulders high he bore
The Jewish people's fame. I saw
Another seven standing by
In honour and in wisdom high
Who helped him with his weighty charge,
It was so heavy and so large.   1440
The writing being of battles fell
And other marvels old as well,
On this account the column there,
Whose use I now to you declare,
Was made of iron and of lead,
For iron is the metal dread
Of Mars, the god of strife and war,
While lead, I tell you now for sure,
Is Saturn's metal, Saturn who
A mighty orbit must go through.   1450
   Then stood forth in row on row
Of those whose histories I know,
Which I shall not in order tell –

Too long on such a host to dwell! –
Those whose fame I shall recall.
I saw there standing first of all
Upon an iron column strong
Painted end to end along
With tigers' blood, the Toulouse poet
Whose name was Statius,* all men know it,   1460
Who on his shoulders bore the fame
Of ancient Thebes, besides the name
Of cruel Achilles, that proud Greek.
And by him stood – no lie I speak –
High on a column of iron true,
Great Homer, with him Dares too,
The Phrygian, Dictys* of Crete
In front, and Lollius, complete
With Guido delle Colonne* and
Geoffrey of Monmouth,* understand?   1470
For each of these, God grant me joy,
Busily penned the fame of Troy.
So mighty was that city's fame,
To write of it was not a game.
In fact, among the six I saw
No little envy spread therefore.
One said that Homer wrote all lies,
His verses being but false surmise
Favouring Greeks to a degree:
It was all fairy tales, said he.   1480
    Iron tin-plated and hence bright
Was the column on whose height
The Latin poet Virgil stood,
Who long maintained with hardihood
The pious Aeneas' mighty fame.
    Next on a copper pillar came
Venus's poet Ovid, who
Publicized the whole world through
The mighty God of Love's great name.
And there he spread abroad his fame   1490
From on the column's top, as high

As I could pierce with my eye;
For all the time this mighty hall
Was growing more wide and long and tall,
And was a thousand times, I saw,
As huge as it had been before.
    Upon a column strongly made
Of iron, next my eye surveyed
The famous poet Lucan,* who
Upon his shoulders gave to view,   1500
So high that I could well behold,
The fame of Caesar and Pompey bold.
And next them all those scholars came
Who wrote of Rome's great deeds and fame,
So many that I haven't time
To state their titles in my rhyme.
    And next there, on a sulphur column,
As if distracted, madly solemn,
Stood Claudian,* I truly tell,
Who wrote of all the fame of hell,   1510
Of Pluto and of Proserpine,*
The queen of torment's dark confine.
Yet why should I inform you more?
That palace was as full, for sure,
Of tellers of tales and histories,
As with rooks' nests lofty trees.
And it would be bewildering
If I recounted everything
They wrote of, and their names as well.
    But while I saw these things I tell   1520
I heard a sudden buzzing sound
Like that in any beehive found
When bees are ready to fly out.
Just such a buzz without a doubt
For all the world it seemed to be.
Looking about, I came to see
A mighty thronging company
Entering the hall tumultuously
From every corner of the earth,

Of every kind and sort of worth   1530
Of folk who live beneath the moon,
Both poor and rich. And just as soon
As they arrived within the hall,
Down on their knees fell one and all
Before this Queen of noble name,
Saying, 'Lovely Lady Fame,
Grant each of us by grace a boon!'
And some of these she granted soon,
And some denied most gracefully,
And others yet, the contrary   1540
Of what they asked she brought about.
But truly I cannot work out
The reason she decided so,
For all those people, as I know,
Although they were diversely served,
A very decent fame deserved;
Fame's like her sister Fortune,* who
Similar things is wont to do.

   Now listen how she satisfied
Those who for her favours cried;   1550
And yet, I say, this company
All told the truth, with never a lie.
'Great Madam,' said they, 'here are we
In supplication come to thee
To beg that thou wilt give us fame
And let our exploits have that name;
In recompense for what we've done,
Make us the gift of high renown!'
   'That I deny,' at once said she,
'You get no high renown from me,   1560
By God! And therefore go your way!'
'Alas!' they wailed, 'And woe the day!
Explain what might your reason be.'
'Because it's not my wish,' said she.
'No one shall speak at all of you,
Not good nor bad, whatever you do.'
Upon which word she then did call

Her messenger, who was in hall,
And told him he at once must find,
On pain of being stricken blind,　　　　　　　1570
Aeolus the God of Wind.
'In Thrace you'll find him; and remind
The god to bring his trumpet here,
Whose various sounds are cloud and clear.
Its name, we know, is Great Renown:
With that he makes the fame well known
Of those whose praise rejoices me.
And tell that god besides that he
Should bring his other clarion
Called Evil Fame in every town,　　　　　　　1580
With which his wont is to defame
Whomever I wish, and do them shame.'
　　This messenger was quickly gone,
And found deep in a cave of stone
Within the country known as Thrace
This Aeolus, with relentless face
Confining with power pitiless
The winds in such extreme distress
That, like wild bears, with growling sound
They roared their agony profound.　　　　　　1590
　　The envoy cried immediately,
'Rise up, and quick as quick can be,
Come to my Lady! And take care
To take your trumpets with you there.
Now hurry up.' So Aeolus told
The sea-god Triton then to hold
His trumpets, and he next let out
A certain wind which blew about
So violently, so loud and high,
That soon in all the wide long sky　　　　　　1600
There was not left a single cloud.
This Aeolus no pause allowed
Until he'd come to the feet of Fame
With that sea-god, Triton by name:
And there he stood, as still as stone.

And soon there came towards the throne
A second mighty company
Of folk who pleaded loud and high:
'Lady, grant us now good fame,
And let our deeds have that great name   1610
Now in honour of chivalry;
And may God bless thy soul so free!
For since we have deserved our fame,
It's right we should receive the same.'
    She answered, 'As I live, you'll fail!
Your virtuous deeds shall not avail
Just now to win renown from me.
But you know what? I here decree
That you shall have an evil fame,
A foul report and fouler name,   1620
Though fair renown you have deserved.
Now off you go: you have been served.
And you, god Aeolus, let me see
You take your trumpet now,' said she,
'The one called Fickle Slander. Blow
Their disrepute, that men shall know
And speak of all their wickedness,
And not their good and worthiness.
For you must trumpet contrary
To deeds of worth and bravery.'   1630
'Alas!' I thought, 'What evil thing
These luckless folk are suffering!
To be so shamed amongst the throng
When surely they have done no wrong!
But Fate cannot be dodged, it's true.'
    So what did Aeolus then do?
He raised his blackened trump of brass
Which fouler than the devil was,
And blew it loudly, as if so
The universe he'd overthrow.   1640
Through every region all around
Went that ghastly trumpet's sound
As fast as cannon-ball from gun

When flames amidst the powder run.
And such a powerful smoke belched out
From that appalling trumpet mouth,
Black, blue and greenish, swarthy red,
As gushes out, when men melt lead,
From the chimney opening.
And then I saw another thing: 1650
The further that the smoke-cloud blew,
The bigger and stronger yet it grew,
Like a river from spring or well;
And it stank like the pit of hell.
Alas! though guiltless, thus was rung
Their shameful name on every tongue!

   A third great company then came
Stepping up to the throne of Fame,
Where down upon their knees they fell,
Exclaiming, 'All of us excel   1660
As people who most certainly
Deserve renown most rightfully.
We pray thee that it may be known
Just as it is, and forth be blown!'
·'I grant it, for it pleases me
That your great deeds be known,' said she.
'Indeed, though foes would do you down,
You shall possess a higher renown
At once than you deserve, I say.
So Aeolus,' said she, 'put away   1670
That trumpet which is black and grim.
Your other trumpet, take out him
Called Great Renown, and blow it so
That round the world their fame shall go
Harmoniously and not too fast,
So that it's known until the last.'
'Most gladly, Lady,' he replied.
His golden trumpet from his side
He drew, and put it to his mouth
And blew it east and west and south   1680
And north, as loud as any thunder,

And all who heard were struck with wonder,
So far it sounded: then it ceased,
And truly, all the breath released
From that fine trumpet's mouth there swelled
As if a pot of balm were held
Inside a basket full of roses,
Scenting their honour in our noses.
   And straight away there caught my eye
A fourth advancing company,   1690
And very few indeed were they:
A single row made their array.
They stood and pleaded, 'Lady bright,
In truth we strove with all our might,
But we have no regard for fame,
So please efface our deeds and name
For love of God, for truly we
Did everything in charity,
And not for gain of any kind.'
Fame answered, 'All you have in mind   1700
Is granted: let your deeds be dead.'
At that I turned and scratched my head,
And saw then a fifth company
Who to this lady bowed the knee,
Bending low before her throne;
And they begged her every one
Not of their good deeds to speak,
Saying they wouldn't give a leek
For fame or noble reputation
Because it was for contemplation   1710
And love of God that they had acted:
By love of fame they weren't attracted.
'What's that? Are you quite mad?' cried she,
'And would you do such charity
And for its doing not win fame?
And do you scorn to have my name?
No! All of you shall live in glory.
Aeolus! Sound out their story
In concord on your trumpet: blow

Their fame that all the world may know,' 1720
She ordered, 'and their deeds may hear.'
And then he blew their fame so clear
Upon his golden clarion,
It crossed the world, went on and on,
Piercing sharp, yet sweetly soft,
And at the last dissolved aloft.

Then came the sixth fine company,
And fast to Fame they raised their cry,
Exclaiming just as I write here,
'Have mercy on us, Lady dear! 1730
To tell it truly as it is,
We have done neither that nor this,
But have been idle all our days,
But each one notwithstanding prays
That he may have as good a name,
As great renown and noble fame,
As those whose deeds were high-aspiring
And who fulfilled their whole desiring
In love or any other thing.
Not one of us had brooch or ring 1740
Or other gift by woman sent;
No lady with her heart's intent
Ever made us friendly cheer
But what might bring us to our bier.
Yet let us to the people seem
Such that the world may of us deem
That women loved us to distraction.
That will produce as good reaction
For us, and heart and spirit please
By counterpoising work and ease, 1750
As if for it we'd worked and fought.
For that is honour dearly bought,
Considering our idleness.
Yet grant thou us still more largess:
Let us be reputed wise,
Honoured and virtuous in men's eyes,
And happy on the field of love.

For love of God, who sits above,
Though we may not have got possession
Of women's bodies, let the impression   1760
Of having done it bring us fame.
Enough that we have such a name!'
Fame said, 'I grant it, by my troth.
Now Aeolus, don't yield to sloth.
Take out your golden trumpet, see,
And blow as they requested me;
So all shall think they earned high praise
Although they practised evil ways.'
So Aeolus made their glory known
And widely through the whole world blown.   1770
    The seventh company then came,
And kneeling down with loud exclaim
Cried, 'Quickly do us, Lady free,
The same favour to the same plea
That to the last lot thou hast done!'
She said, 'Fie on you every one!
You sluggish swine, you lazy wretches,
Full of rotten torpid tetches!
What? Lying thieves, how could you ask
For fame, and then in glory bask   1780
Without deserving, and not care?
You should be hanged for that, I swear!
For you are like the fagged-out cat
Who longed for fish; but you know what?
He couldn't bear to wet his claws.
May bad luck grip you by the jaws,
And me as well if I agree
To favour your posterity!
Now Aeolus, you King of Thrace,
Go blow this lot a rotten grace   1790
At once!' said she, 'And you know how?
Do just as I instruct you now.
Say: "These men want an honoured name,
But haven't done a thing for fame,
Not one good deed, yet they'd persuade

The world Isolde* couldn't evade
Inviting them to serve love's turn!"
A slattern grinding at a quern
Would be too good to ease their heart.'
Aeolus leapt up with a start   1800
And on his blackened trumpet blew
A sounding din, I swear to you,
As loud as bellowing gale in hell,
With comic blasts which, truth to tell,
Were just as many as grimaces
Upon a crowd of monkeys' faces.
All round the world the discords went,
And everyone who heard gave vent,
As if quite mad, to laughs and shouts,
Such fun they made of those poor louts.   1810
    Then came another company
Who had performed more treachery
And done more harm and wickedness
Than any living soul could guess.
They prayed to her for virtuous fame,
And begged her not to bring them shame,
But have them praised and well renowned.
In the appropriate trumpet sound.
'No, that would be,' said she, 'a vice.
I know my justice isn't nice,   1820
But all the same, I don't feel pleased,
And therefore you shall not be eased.'
    Next came leaping in a gang
Who laid about with thwack and bang,
Hitting men upon the head
And making people howl with dread
Throughout the palace. 'Lady dear!'
They cried, 'We're men, as you can hear.
To tell the truth and get it done,
We're horrid villains every one,   1830
Who take delight in wickedness
As good folk do in righteousness.
We love to be renowned as knaves

Whom brutal roguery depraves;
And so we line up to request
That you our proper fame attest
Exactly as it really is.'
Fame said, 'Of course I grant you this:
But who are you, with stripe upon
Your stocking and a bell* upon   1840
Your cope, to make me such a plea?'
'Madam, to tell the truth,' said he,
'I am the man of vile renown
Who burned the temple of Isis down
In Athens, city by the sea.'
'And why did you do that?' asked she.
He said, 'I swear, my Lady Fame,
I wished to have a famous name
Like other people in the town,
Although they all won great renown   1850
By noble deeds and moral powers.
I thought as great fame should be ours,
We evil men, for wickedness,
As good men have for righteousness.
Since fair renown I cannot know,
The other one I won't forego;
And so to interest Lady Fame,
I set the temple all aflame.
Now if thou truly wouldst rejoice,
Have our fame blown with trumpet noise!'   1860
'Gladly!' said she. 'Aeolus!
You hear what they implore of us?'
Said he, 'My Lady, yes, I hear.
By God, I'll trumpet loud and clear!'
He took his pitch-black trumpet fast,
And puffed and blew with mighty blast
Until the world's end heard the sound.

   And at that point I swivelled round
Because it seemed someone* behind
Me spoke with words both good and kind,   1870
Saying, 'Friend, what is your name?

And have you ventured here for fame?'
'No, truly,' answered I, 'my friend.
God save my soul, for no such end
Did I come hither, by my head!
It will suffice when I am dead
That no one falsely quotes my name.
My right worth I myself best claim,
For what I suffer, what I think,
Shall wholly be my own to drink,   1880
As surely, for the greater part,
As I know my poet's art.'
'But why come here then?' questioned he.
I said, 'I'll tell you openly
The reason for my being here:
Of deeds or news I well might hear,
Or novel thing, I don't know what,
Some great event, of this or that,
Of love, or other happy thing.
For truly, he who chanced to bring   1890
Me hither well instructed me
That in this place I'd hear and see
Extraordinary goings-on:
But it's not the things being done
I chiefly mean.' Said he, 'Oh no?'
'By God!' I answered, 'No, not so.
For ever since my wits matured,
My mind has truly been assured
That many people longed for fame
In different ways to praise their name.   1900
But certainly I knew not how
Or where Fame lived until just now,
Nor did I know her form or feature,
Her way of life or living nature,
Or her style of dealing doom,
Until to this place I had come.'
'Then what about those new events
You mentioned with such eloquence
Of which you've heard?' he said to me.

114

'No matter now, for well I see   1910
Exactly what you want to hear.
Come forth, and stay no longer here,
And I shall faithfully direct
You where you may indeed inspect
And listen to such goings-on.'
   It wasn't long before we'd gone
Out of the castle, I declare.
Then saw I in a valley there
Close by beneath the castle wall
The House of Daedalus.* Men call   1920
It Labyrinth, for never house
Was made so wholly marvellous,
Or with such quaint designing wrought.
For all the time, as swift as thought
It whirled around, that mighty hall,
And never once stayed still at all.
And from it came so strange a noise
That had it stood upon the Oise*
Men could have heard it easily
As far as Rome, most certainly.   1930
For all the world the din I heard,
As all around the place it whirred,
Was like the roaring of a stone
When from a catapult it's thrown.
And all this house of which I tell you
Was built with twigs, red, brownish yellow
And green; and some were whittled white
As when men fashion cages right,
Or are the manufacturers
Of baskets or of panniers.   1940
What with the swishing of the twigs,
The moans and squeaks and creaking jigs,
The house was full of clamourings
Of movement and of other things.
It had as many entrances
As there are leaves upon the trees
In summer when they bloom with green;

115

And on its roof were to be seen
More than a thousand holes, I know,
To let the sound out from below.   1950
All day the doors were open wide,
At morning, noon and eventide;
Wide too, at night, the doorways stood.
There was no porter there who could
Admit good news or false report.
There was no rest of any sort
Within, but what was still infused
With shouted or with whispered news.
The house's corners, all its angles,
Were full of chitter-chatter jangles   1960
Of wars and peace and marriages,
Of rest and work, and voyages,
Of suffering, of death and life,
Of love and hate, accord and strife,
Of praise, of loss and then of gain,
Health, sickness, then of cure again;
Of tempests and of zephyrs mild,
Plague deaths of men and creatures wild;
Of various sudden transmutations
Of circumstances and locations;   1970
Of trust and doubt and jealousy,
Of wit and folly, victory,
Of plenty and of great starvation,
Of trade, of dearth, of ruination,
Of good rule and bad governments,
Of fire and various accidents.
   This house of which I tell you all
Was certainly by no means small,
For it was sixty miles in length.
Although the timber had no strength,   1980
Yet it was founded to endure
As long as Chance exerts her lure,
Who gives all news her mothering,
As sea is mother of well and spring;
And it was fashioned like a cage.

'In all my life, I will engage,
Such a house I never saw,'
Said I and, pondering it with awe,
I suddenly became aware
My Eagle friend was close by there   1990
Perched upon a stone on high.
So quickly to him then went I
And spoke the following: 'I pray
That with me for a while you'll stay
For love of God, and help me see
What wonders in this place may be.
For I may learn by happy chance
Some good, and so my mind enhance
With pleasing truth, before I leave.'
'By Peter, that I shall achieve!'   2000
Said he, 'And that is why I stay.
And one thing I am bound to say:
Unless I show the way to you,
There's nothing you could ever do
To gain admission, without doubt,
Because it whirls so fast about.
But seeing Jove in bounteous measure,
As I have said, will grant you pleasure
Finally in all these things –
Unusual sights and happenings –   2010
To help you fight your dolefulness;
And seeing he pities your distress,
Which you combat so manfully,
And so well knows you utterly
To have surrendered hope of bliss,
Since Lady Fortune did amiss,
Making that fruit, your peace of heart,
Rotten and ready to burst apart –
He through his mighty merit will
In small degree your wish fulfil.   2020
For he expressly ordered me –
And I obey, as you shall see –
To help you on with all my might,

Equipping you with guidance right,
To hear all news of consequence:
You'll promptly learn of such events.'
Upon those words he swiftly rose
And, seizing me between his toes,
He through a window in the wall
Conducted me, as I recall –   2030
And then that house's whirling stopped;
All movement there to nothing dropped –
And set me down upon the floor.
Such milling crowds of folk galore
As I saw roaming all about,
Some in the hall, and some without,
Were never, nor yet will be, seen:
In all the world have never been
So many brought to birth by Nature,
Nor yet died so many a creature;   2040
So scarcely in the whole wide place
Could I secure a foot's breadth space.
And every person I saw there
Was whispering in another's ear
Some novel tidings secretly,
Or else was talking openly
As thus: 'What's happened? Have you heard?
And do you know the latest word?'
'No,' said the other, 'tell me what.'
The other told him this and that,   2050
And swore that all of it was true.
'He says so' and 'He's going to do';
'He's at it now!' 'I heard some chat';
'You'll find it's true!' 'I'll bet on that!'
Yes, all who on this planet dwell
Would not possess the craft to tell
The many things that there I heard
By open speech or whispered word.
But most astonishing of all,
When one heard something, I recall,   2060
Straight to another man he went

118

And immediately gave vent
To all that he had just been told
Before the yarn was two ticks old,
And by the way he told the tale,
He magnified the news's scale
And made it bigger than before.
And when he left him, what was more,
He drew a breath and quickly met
A third man, and before he let   2070
A moment pass, he told him too,
And whether it was false or true,
Each time he told it to a man
His news was more and stranger than
It was before. Thus north and south
Went all the news from mouth to mouth,
Each time increasing more and more,
Like fire that starts to glow and draw
From sparks that accidentally flash,
Until a city's burnt to ash.   2080
And when the tale was fully sprung
By growing greater on each tongue
That told it, then at once it tried
To find a gap and fly outside;
But if it failed there it would try
To creep out by some crack, then fly
Away at once. While watching there,
I saw two rising to the air,
A falsehood and a serious truth
By chance at one time coming both   2090
And striving for a window space.
Colliding in that narrow place,
Each one was hindered, as it tried
To make its own escape outside,
By the other one and, jostling there,
They started shouting, I declare.
'Let me go first!' 'No, no, let me!
I promise you most faithfully,
On condition that you do,

That I shall never go from you,   2100
But swear to be your own true brother!
We shall so mingle with each other
That no man, even in a rage,
Shall have just one, but must engage
The two of us, like it or not,
Come day or night, come cold or hot,
Be we loud or softly sounded.'
Thus saw I false and true confounded,
Flying up in each report.
   So out of holes there squeezed and fought   2110
Each bit of news, and went to Fame,
Who gave to each report its name
According to its disposition,
And fixed its life-span by permission:
Some to wax and wane quite soon
Like the beautiful white moon,
Then disappear. There might you see
Winged wonders flying furiously,
Twenty thousand rushing out
As Aeolus blew them about.   2120
Lord! Non-stop in that house I saw
Sailors and pilgrims by the score,
Their satchels stuffed brimful with lies
Mixed up with truth and some surmise,
And each, moreover, by himself.
O many a thousand times twelve
Did I perceive these pardoners,
Couriers too and messengers
With boxes crammed with falsities
As full as bottles are of lees.   2130
And as I swiftly moved and went
About fulfilling my intent,
Obtaining knowledge and diversion
By getting news in many a version
About some land of which I'd heard –
Of that I shall not say a word:
Truly, no need, for others sing

It better than my minstrelling;
For soon or late, without a doubt,
Like sheaves from a barn, all must out –   2140
There struck my ear a mighty din
In a hall-corner far within,
Where news of love and all its ways
Was being told: thither my gaze
I bent and saw men running there
As fast as ever they could, I swear.
And all exclaimed, 'What thing is that?'
And some replied, 'We don't know what.'
And as they scrambled in a heap,
Those behind them tried to leap   2150
And clamber over them on high,
Raising prying nose and eye,
And treading on each other's heels
And stamping, as men do on eels.
At last I saw a person there
Of whose true name I'm not aware.
But certainly he seemed to be
A man of great authority ...*

The Parliament of Birds

INTRODUCTION TO
'THE PARLIAMENT OF BIRDS'

The poem was written in 1382-3, and D. S. Brewer (*The Parlement of Foulys*, Manchester University Press, 1972, p.3) thinks it was ready for St Valentine's Day, 1383. Determined postulants of theories that it was written for this or that royal betrothal might perhaps be discouraged by the poem's suggestion that the aristocratic lovers have the worst of the argument. More happily, 'The Parliament of Birds' may be regarded as a festive poem composed for St Valentine's Day, probably to please a patron and his or her courtly circle. The main sources, which are better described by Robinson's phrase 'literary borrowings', are the *Somnium Scipionis* of Cicero, as commented on by Macrobius, for the opening; Boccaccio's *Teseide* for the description of the Garden of Love and its presiding goddess, Venus (ll.183-294); and the *De Planctu Naturae* (Nature's Complaint) of Alanus de Insulis for the description of Nature and the birds (ll.298-371). The form is the familiar medieval one of the love debate, incorporating the *demande d'amour*.

Following five stanzas of confidential personal opening come two hundred and fifty lines of noble lyricism, as Chaucer gives notice of his theme. The lofty advice of Scipio to 'sustain the common profit' is planted so that it may be applied in the Garden of Love, to whose gates the dead sage guides the living poet. Above the gates are inscribed two Dantesque welcomes, of which the first (ll.127-33) seems to be addressed to those capable of happy natural love, and the second (ll.134-40) to those inclined to submit to the extraordinary rituals and emotional demands of courtly love. The theme has already broadened, and it becomes broader still when, nearest in favour to the lovely half-naked presiding goddess, Priapus erect is observed. The catalogue of lovers whose love ended in disaster (ll.281–94), coming so soon after, forbids anticipation of a happy celebration of St Valentine's Day, and we remember that one of Jove's complaints against Chaucer in 'The House of Fame' was that he did not write of happy loves.

The Venus celebrated by both Boccaccio and Chaucer presides over all three chief kinds of Love: married love (which presumably includes 'natural' love), courtly love and lust. Since Scipio offers certain damnation to the lustful (l.79), and the uses of the particular trees seen in the Garden of Love (ll.176–82) seem on the whole to provide furnishings for disastrous passion rather than for harmonious love, it appears that Chaucer is preparing, by example and allegorical suggestion, for a complex and mixed upshot, even though his setting (ll.204–210) remains rhapsodically idealized.

The birds assembled for the love debate are classified in a hierarchical system – birds of prey, water-birds, seed-birds and worm-birds – which parallels human social organization, though probably not exactly: serfs, yeomen, merchants and priests cannot be specified, though royalty and nobles can. The first love declaration, by the royal tercel, reveals aristocratic presumption mixed with what the eagle means to be the total humility required from the courtly lover. *Choosing*, by the man, should mean selecting a woman to whom he offers obedience and service – without the assumption that such choice ought to determine her response, and also debar other contestants for her hand (ll.435–441). Thus the courtesy which at first seemed to be the poem's staple force declines, and the debate continues with the gloves off.

In an increasingly comic atmosphere aristocratic pretension, supported in a moderate way even by Nature herself (ll.624–37), goes on the defensive against the lower classes of birds, who in their different ways recommend the harmonious, natural love that Chaucer suggests most people desire and achieve. Only the turtle-dove urges the pure ideal of everlasting fidelity to an indifferent loved one (ll.582–8); and in the conclusion, in which the female eagle imposes a pause of a year on her suitors, this possibility is left open, as it is for the King of Navarre and his lords at the end of *Love's Labour's Lost*. But for

The Parliament of Birds

the masses, happy singing and mating affirm the grand human
purpose of the feast of St Valentine's Day. In the last thirty lines,
the lyricism surges afresh to conclude a beautifully compressed
and happy poem.

THE PARLIAMENT OF BIRDS

So short is life, so long to learn is art!*
So hard the trial, so keen our least success!
Our perilous joys, so swift to leave the heart!
All this I link with Love, and I confess
Myself astounded by his artfulness,
Which brings such pain that when I pause and think,
I'm hardly certain whether I float or sink.   7

For though I know not Love in very deed,
Nor how he pays the folk who've earned their hire,
It happens that in books I often read
About his miracles and cruel ire,
And resolution to be Lord and Sire:
And since his blows are fierce, 'God save that Lord!'
Is all I dare say – not another word!   14

I read, as I informed you, many a book,
For pleasure or instruction, understand?
But why go on like this? I chanced to look
Not long since at a book the scribal hand
Of which was ancient. This I keenly scanned
In search of something special that I sought;
All day I read that book with eager thought.   21

For as in ancient fields they say it's true
That new corn strongly grows from year to year,
So truly out of ancient volumes too
New knowledge comes that learned men can hear.
But let my purpose in this now appear.

The Parliament of Birds

The reading gave me such high pleasure in it
That that whole day seemed scarce to last a minute. 28

This book, as I should like you all to know,
Had this full title which I now shall tell:
Scipio's Dream by Tullius Cicero.*
It had seven chapters featuring heaven and hell
And earth, and all the souls that therein dwell,
Concerning which, as briefly as I may,
The meaning and main drift I shall convey. 35

How Scipio came to Africa it tells,*
And meeting Masinissa there, entwined
Him in his arms for joy. It further tells
Their blissful talk, and how they called to mind
Old Africanus as the day declined,
So that at night his well-loved grandsire came
While Scipio slept, appearing in his dream. 42

Next it recounts how from his starry place
His grandsire showed him Carthage far below,
First telling Scipio with kindly grace
That any man in whom the virtues grow
Who loves the common good that all men know,
Learned or lay, shall dwell at last in bliss
In that far place where joy eternal is. 49

Then Scipio asked him if the earthly dead
Have life and dwelling in another place.
'For certain, yes,' old Africanus said,
Affirming that our worldly lifetime's space
Is but a kind of death, whatever grace
We show; that righteous souls at death go free
To heaven. He showed him then the Galaxy. 56

He showed him next the little earth down here,
So small beside the heavens' quantity;
And then he showed him all the nine spheres;

And after that the heavenly tunes heard he
That issue from those turning spheres thrice three,
The source of music and of melody
On earth below, and cause of harmony.*   63

He then advised him, earth being small and slight
And full of torment and of hard-won grace,
He should not linger in this world's delight.
He said that after a certain period's space
Each star would be restored to that same place
Where it began, and all works of mankind
On earth be lost to the eternal mind.   70

Then Scipio begged his grandsire to explain
How he might reach the realm of heavenly bliss.
He said, 'Since you're immortal, first sustain
The common profit: seeking that, employ
Your efforts and persuasion; thus enjoy
A swift arrival in the well-loved place
Where purest souls abide in bliss and grace.   77

'But breakers of the law, when they are dead,
And lecherous people, I must make it plain,
Shall whirl about on earth in constant dread
And agony, while ages pass in pain;
And then, forgiven their wicked deeds, they'll gain
The right to enter that delightful place,
To which may God send you with all his grace.'   84

The day began to fail, and gloomy night,
Which interrupts all beasts' activity,
Deprived me of my book through lack of light,
And I prepared for bed in gravity,
Replete with thoughts of much solemnity;
For I had that which I did not desire,
But not that thing which I did most desire.   91

But finally my spirit at the last,

Exhausted by the labours of the day,
Took rest and lodged me in a slumber fast.
And in that sleep I dreamed that where I lay,
Old Africanus, in the same array
That Scipio before had seen him wear,
Had come, and by my bed was standing there.   98

In sleep the weary hunter's dreaming mind
Travels from bed to forests that he knows;
The justice dreams how lawsuits loose and bind;
The carter dreams how trade by wagon goes;
The rich man dreams of gold; the knight fights foes;
The sick man dreams of drinking draughts of wine;
The lover dreams he's won his lady fine.   105

I cannot say the cause was that I'd read
Of Africanus first, and therefore took
Him to my dream, there standing by my bed;
But thus said he, 'So graciously you look,
And kindly, on my old and tattered book,
For which Macrobius' love was more than slight,
That something of your pains I shall requite.'   112

O Venus, blissful lady sweet and fine,
Whose torch subdues all those you wish to arrest,
Whose influence made me dream this dream of mine,
Be my support in this, for you may best!
And since I truly saw you north-north-west*
As I began to pen my dream at length,
To write and rhyme correctly, give me strength!   119

This Africanus forthwith took me out
And led me to a double gate which brought
Us to a park with mossed stone walled about.
Above that gate in mighty letters wrought,
Two sets of lines had been inscribed, I thought,
One either side, but both quite different.
And I shall now say fully what they meant.   126

'Through me men go into that blissful place*
Where hearts revive and deadly wounds have cure;
Through me men travel to the well of grace,
Where green and lusty May shall ever endure.
This is the way to fortune good and pure.
Be happy, reader, and throw off your woe:
I'm open. Enter now and quickly go!'   133

'Through me men go,' then said the other side,
'To suffer deadly stabbing from the spear
Which both Disdain and shamefast Danger guide.
Of leaves and fruit, trees here are always bare.
This stream will lead you to the joyless weir
Where fish are caught up, trapped and left to dry:
Avoidance is the only remedy.'   140

In gold and black those lines were written there,
And both made me amazedly behold,
For one continually increased my fear,
And the other filled my heart with spirit bold.
One warmed me well, the other chilled with cold.
No wit had I, being full of doubt, to choose,
Go in or flee, myself to save or lose.   147

Exactly like a piece of iron set
Between two lodestones of force parallel,
Which has no power to move this way or that –
One magnet tries to pull, the other repel –
Was I, in doubt if I should do as well
To enter or leave: till African, my guide,
Took me and shoved me in that entrance wide,   154

And said, 'I see it written in your face,
Your error, though you tell it not to me;
But do not fear to come into this place.
Those lines speak not to you unless you be
Of Love the servant and the devotee.
But you have lost your taste for love, I see,

As sick men have for sweet and savoury.   161

'But all the same, although your spirit be low,
Yet what you cannot do you yet may see.
For many a man who cannot stand a throw
Takes pleasure at a wrestling match to be,
To judge who wins, this or that other he:
And if you have the skill of writing men,
I'll show you subject matter for your pen.'   168

And thereupon my hand in his he seized,
Which solaced me, and then we went in fast.*
And Lord, how glad I was and how well pleased!
For everywhere I looked, my eyes were cast
On trees whose foliage would for ever last,
Each kind as fresh and green as emerald
In its own way, a pleasure to behold.   175

The builder's oak tree and the hardy ash;
The elm for stakes and coffins for the dead;
Box for pipe-making; holly for whips to lash;
The fir for masts; for grief the cypress dread;
The yew for bows; poplar for shafts smooth-made;
The peaceful olive and the drinker's vine;
The victor's palm; the laurel, augury's sign.   182

A garden full of blossoming boughs I saw
Beside a river in a verdant mead,
Where lives abundant sweetness evermore,
With flowers white and blue, yellow and red,
And cool spring-water streams, by no means dead,
But swimming with little fishes darting light
With fins of red and scales of silver bright.   189

I heard the birds on every branch there singing
With angel-voices in their harmony;
And some were busy with their chicks' upbringing.
The little rabbits in their games in glee

Ran fast; and all around me I could see
The timid roe, the buck, the hart, the hind,
Squirrels and creatures small of gentle kind.   196

I heard stringed instruments in sweet accord
Played with such ravishing melodiousness
That God, the All-Creator and the Lord,
Never heard better music, as I guess.
And then a wind — it scarcely could be less —
Made in the leafy green a murmuring soft
In concord with the bird-song there aloft.   203

The air of that sweet place so temperate was
That never came complaint of heat or cold;
There also thrived all wholesome spice and grass;
And there no man became diseased or old;
And yet delight waxed there a thousandfold
Beyond the telling. Never came the night,
But everlasting day stayed clear in sight.   210

Under a tree beside a spring I saw
Cupid our Lord his arrows forge and file,*
And at his feet his bow ready to draw;
Desire, his daughter, tempered all the while
The arrow-heads in the spring, thus with her guile
Fixing the use to which they would be put —
Some to kill and some to wound and cut.   217

Then was I aware of Pleasure straight away,*
Adornment too, Liking and Courtesy,
And Craftiness that has the power to sway
Or force a man to foolish errancy —
I tell you truly, most deformed was she.
And by himself beneath an oak I spied
Delight, who had Good Breeding by his side.   224

Beauty I saw there, bare of all attire,
And Youth, replete with fun and jollity,

Foolhardiness and Flattery and Desire,
Report and Bribery, another three –
Their names shall not be uttered here by me! –
And up on jasper pillars huge and long
I saw a brazen temple firm and strong.   231

About that temple troops of ladies danced
Unceasingly, and beautiful they were
Themselves, though some by lovely dress enhanced;
In flowing gowns they danced with long loose hair:
That was their endless duty year by year.
And on the temple, doves most white and fair
I saw there perching, many a hundred pair.   238

In solemn calm before the temple door
Sat Lady Peace, a curtain in her hand,
And at her side, remarkably demure,
The Lady Patience sitting there I scanned,
With face all pale, upon a hill of sand.*
But closest of all, inside and outside too,
Appeared Behest and Art with all their crew.   245

Within the temple sighs as hot as fire
I heard with murmur heaving to and fro,
Sighs engendered by profound desire,
Which were the reason that each altar so
Burned up with flame afresh: that made me know
That all the woe they felt so piercingly
Came from the bitter goddess Jealousy.   252

As I went on, I saw in pride of place
The god Priapus* in the selfsame state
As when the donkey brayed him to disgrace
One night. He held his sceptre there up straight,
And men were trying with exertion great
To put upon his head fresh flowers new
In garlands bright of variegated hue.   259

And in a secret corner in delight
Venus I found, and Wealth who kept her door,
A noble person, haughty to the sight.
The place was dark, but farther on I saw
By glimmering light, enough to see, no more,
Where on a bed of gold she lay at rest
Until the hot sun fell towards the west.   266

Her golden hair was banded with a thread
Of gilt, and all unbraided as she lay;
And naked from the breast up to the head
Men might behold her, and it's true to say
The rest was vestured in a pleasing way
With a Valence kerchief woven fine enough –
No better cover from any thicker stuff!   273

The place gave off a thousand odours sweet.
Bacchus,* the god of wine, was sitting there,
With Ceres next, who lets the hungry eat,
And midst of all there lay that Cyprian rare
To whom there knelt and prayed a youthful pair,
Seeking her help: and thus I left her lying,
And deeper in the temple came to spying   280

That there, to spite Diana, goddess chaste,*
A mass of broken bows hung on the wall
Of girls whose service with her ran to waste:
And painted everywhere within that hall
Were their sad tales; of which I shall recall
A few:* Callisto, Atalanta and
Others whose names I cannot now command.   287

Semiramis, Candace and Hercules,
Byblis, Dido, Thisbe and Pyramus,
Tristan, Isolde, Paris, Achilles,
Cleopatra, Helen, Troilus,
Scylla and the mother of Romulus,
Were all depicted on the farther side

The Parliament of Birds

With all their love, and in what plight they died. 294

When I had come again into the park
I spoke of first, which was so lush and green,
I walked, to ease my mind of stories dark.
And then I saw her sitting, lo! a queen
Whose brilliance, as the sun in summer sheen
Surpasses that of stars, by far outshone
The beauty of beings created, every one. 301

Yes, in a glade upon a hill of flowers
There sat that noble goddess men call Nature.
All made of branches were her halls and bowers,
Designed as she had cast their form and feature;
Nor was there a bird, a true begotten creature,
That was not prompt to come within her sight
To hear her and accept her judgements right. 308

For this was on Saint Valentine's feast day,*
When all birds come their mates to pick and take.
Of every breed that mankind knows were they,
And hence a mighty din they there did make,
And earth and air and tree and every lake
Were so thick-crowded there was hardly space
For me to stand, so full was all that place. 315

Alan's *Complaint of Nature** makes it clear
Exactly how she looked in dress and face,
And just as Alan says was Nature here.
This noble empress, fair and full of grace,
Bade every bird take up his proper place
As they were wont to always every year
Upon Saint Valentine's Day, assembling there. 322

That is to say, the birds of prey were set
In highest place, and next came those more small,
Like birds who followed Nature's laws and ate
Such things as worms whose names I do not call;

And lowest in the glade sat water-fowl.
But on the green sat birds that live on seed,
So many, it was strange to see indeed.   329

There might a man the royal eagle find,
Who with his fierce sharp look pierces the sun,*
And other eagles of a lesser kind,
About whom writers' tales are deftly spun.
There was the tyrant with his feathers dun
And grey, I mean the goshawk, fell in deed
To birds with his outrageous ire and greed.   336

The gentle falcon, who clutches in his claws
The hand of kings; the sturdy sparrowhawk too,
Foe of the quail; the merlin who explores
Ways all the time the small lark to pursue;
There was the meek-eyed dove full in my view;
The angry swan, of his coming death the singer;
The owl as well, of death the omen-bringer;   343

The crane, that giant, his cry a trumpet's blow;
The chough, that thief; the magpie with his chatter;
The mocking jay; the heron, to every eel a foe;
The treacherous lapwing, prone to falsely flatter;
The starling, who betrays all secret matter;
The robin tame; the kite, that cowardly bird;
The cock, that clock in little hamlets heard;   350

The sparrow, Venus' son; the nightingale,
Whose singing summons forth the green leaves new;
The swallow, murderer of the creatures small
Whose honey comes from flowers fresh of hue;
The married turtle with her heart so true;
The peacock with his plumage angel-bright;
The pheasant, scorner of the cock by night;   357

The watchful goose; the cuckoo ever unkind;
The parrot, always full of lechery;

The Parliament of Birds

The drake, destroyer of his own true kind;
The stork, avenger of adultery;
The fiery cormorant, full of gluttony;
The raven wise; the crow with voice of care;
The long-lived thrush; the frosty fieldfare.   364

How shall I tell you? Birds of every kind
Which on this earth have feather, form and stature,
Assembled in that place you well might find
Attending on the noble goddess Nature.
And earnest moves were made by every creature
To take or choose in manner delicate,
With her accord, his helpmeet or his mate.   371

But to the point. In Nature's hand she held
A formel* eagle, quite the loveliest
She'd found in her creations. She excelled
In grace and beauty of the tenderest,
And was of every virtue well possessed,
So much indeed that Nature felt it bliss
To gaze on her and give her beak a kiss.   378

Nature, vice-gerent of our mighty Lord,
Who poises hot and cold, and moist and dry,*
And heavy and light in mutual accord,
With gentle voice began to speak and say:
'You birds, attend to this my judgement, pray!
To please you now in furthering your need,
I shall speak out, and with the utmost speed.   385

'You all know well that on Saint Valentine's Day,
By laws of mine and by my government,
You come to choose – and after fly away –
Your mates, by me impelled on passion's bent.
In this my rule of law brooks no dissent,
Nor would I break it all this world to win.
The bird that is most excellent shall begin.   392

'The tercel* eagle so well known to you,
That royal bird above you in degree,
Wise, excellent, discreet and steel-true,
Whom I created as you well may see
In all his parts as it delighted me –
No need to detail them to you – he shall
In making choice of mate be first of all.   399

'And after him in order you shall choose
As you desire, according to your kind:
As Chance determines, you shall win or lose.
God send the bird by Love's trap most confined
The mate who sighs for him with strongest mind!'
Then cried she to the tercel: 'Son, to you
The right to be the first to choose is due.   406

'But all the same, there is a firm condition
Binding on all who make their choices here:
A female must agree the proposition
Of him who wants to be her husband dear.
Our custom is just so, from year to year,
And that is why all birds have special grace
This blissful time in coming to this place.'   413

With head inclined, and humbly delicate,
The royal tercel quickly made the start:
'I address my sovereign lady, not my mate.
I choose, and choose with mind and will and heart,
The one you hold, so fair in every part.
I'll serve her always; hers alone am I,
Whatever she does to make me live or die.   420

'And thus I beg her mercy and her grace,
Because she is my lady sovereign;
Or let me end my life now, in this place!
For truly, long I cannot live in pain,
My heart so bleeds, being cut in every vein.
Regard my faith, have pity on my woe,

My dearest heart, because I suffer so.   427

'And if to her I should be found untrue,
Or disobedient, wilful-negligent,
Or boastful, or take on a lover new,
I beg you this may be my punishment:
That by these birds I may be ripped and rent
The very day that ever she shall find
Me false or cruel, unnatural to my kind.   434

'And since I love her more than others do,
Although she never promised me her love,
She should be mine by force of mercy true:
No other claim on her can I approve.
Never shall pain or woe make me remove,
However far she fly, my humble vow!
Say what you will, my plea is ended now.'   441

Just as the fresh red rose colours anew
Against the sun when summer comes with bliss,
So deepened then the formel's tender hue
Of feature as she listened to all this.
She neither answered well nor spoke amiss,
So gravely shy was she, till Nature said,
'Daughter, be sure there is no cause for dread.'   448

A lower-ranking tercel came to sue,
At once exclaiming, 'That shall never be!
For by Saint John, I love her more than you –
Or at the least, I love as fervently.
I've served her longer in my own degree,
So if her favour to long love were shown,
The just reward would come to me alone.   455

'I say besides, if she find me untrue,
Cruel or prattling, prone to disagree
Or jealous, hang me by the neck! This too:
If I fail to serve her loyally,

As well as all my wits can counsel me
Ever to guard her honour, then may she
Take from me life and all my property!'   462

Then up spoke tercel eagle number three:
'Now sirs, you see how time grows precious here!
For every bird that's present longs to be
Gone with his mate or with his lady dear.
And even Nature, waiting, will not hear
The half of what I long to say, for I
Am bound to speak, or else for sorrow die.   469

'I brag not of long service as a thing,
But I could die of grief as well today
As one whose twenty winters' languishing
Had killed him off. Indeed I'd say
Six months, no more, of loyal service may
Please better, if the right man were to come,
Than ages of good service done by some.   476

'Not for myself I say it, for I can
Not serve my lady pleasingly at all;
But I believe I am her truest man,
In wish to cheer her happiest of all.
In brief, till ugly death grips me in thrall,
I shall be hers whether I sleep or wake,
And true in all heart's thought for her sweet sake.'   483

In all my life, since that day I was born,
No man with leisure and knowledge of Love's word
In speech and gesture, so I dare be sworn,
Such pleas of love or other things had heard
As those so gently made by every bird.
And from the morning did the speaking last
Till evening, when the sun descended fast.   490

So loudly through the air the bird-calls flew
To be set free – 'Have done, and let us go!' –

The Parliament of Birds

I thought the forest would have burst in two.
'Come on!' they cried, 'You'll bring us all to woe!
This curst debate must stop! When will it so?
How can a judge without a sign of proof
Resolve the case on any bird's behoof?'   497

Then cried the goose, the duck, the cuckoo too,
'Kek-kek! Quack quack! Cuckoo! Cuckoo!' so high
That with the din my ears were riddled through.
'All this,' the goose said, 'isn't worth a fly!
I've got a thorough cure for it, have I:
Whoever's pleased or cross, my vote I cast
For water-birds, and do it loud and fast!'   504

'And I for worm-birds!' the daft cuckoo cried,
'For I shall on my own authority
For benefit of all birds so decide,
Because it's charity to set us free!'
The turtle-dove then spoke: 'If you agree
A bird should speak, perhaps he'd better not.
So hold your peace and wait a while, by God!   511

'I am a seed-bird, and among the least,
As well I know, and meagre is my skill.
A bird should rather keep his tongue at rest
Than in such complex matters meddle ill,
If wisdom he can neither speak nor trill.
When not appointed judge, to act as such
Corrupts the self while irking others much.'   518

Nature, who always hearkened to the din
The ignorant made while muttering behind,
Said eloquently, 'Rein your wild tongues in!
A course I hope that I shall quickly find
To free you from this turmoil, unconfined.
I rule we call on one bird of each kind
To give a verdict, state the common mind.'   525

This course of action was approved by all
The birds, and naturally the birds of prey
Were first to pick the one to whom should fall
The task. The tercel falcon was to say
What was their thought, their judgement to convey.
To offer it to Nature then he went,
And she accepted him with glad consent.   532

Thus spoke the falcon in a manner clear:
'It would be hard to prove or to assess
Who most adores this noble formel here,
For each one can a special pleading press
Which will resist all talk and cleverness.
I cannot see debate will make things right,
And so it seems it must be done by fight.'   539

'All ready!' cried those eagles, three as one.
'No, sirs!' the falcon said, 'I'm bound to say
You do me wrong; my judgement is not done!
Be not aggrieved, my gentle sirs, I pray.
Though you may wish it, that is not the way.
We are the ones who have this case in hand,
And to the judges' deeming you must stand.   546

'So therefore, peace! I'm sure my mind and wit
Persuade me that the very worthiest
In knighthood, he who longest practised it,
The highest-ranked, in blood the lordliest,
Is fittest for her, if she thinks it best.
And she must know, and know it easily,
Which of the eagles is the chosen he.'   553

The water-birds then all put head to head,
And after brief discussion pertinent,
When every bird his mouthful big had said,
They all agreed with frank and true assent,
Saying, 'The goose, so gently eloquent,
Who so desires to spell out what we need,
Shall speak our mind. God grant her fortune's speed!'   560

144

The Parliament of Birds

So then for all those water-birds the goose
Began to speak, and in her cackling way
Said, 'Peace! Our reasons I shall now produce.
So pay attention, hear what I shall say!
My wit is sharp; I do not like delay.
I say I tell him, though he were my brother,
If she won't love him, let him love another!'   567

'Lo, hear this perfect logic of a goose!
Ill may she fare!' then said the sparrowhawk.
'Lo, what it is to have a tongue so loose!
By God, you fool, far better not to talk
Than show your folly by a silly squawk.
His wit can't help him, neither can his will:
It's truly said, "A fool cannot stay still." '   574

At this the well-bred birds laughed one and all.
The seed-birds chose their speaker straight away,
The turtle-dove. To her they made their call
About the matter, begged her to convey
The sober truth in what she had to say.
She answered she would show her clear intent,
And faithfully explain just what she meant.   581

'No, God forbid! A lover seek to change?'
The turtle-dove* cried out, in shame going red,
'For though his lady evermore be strange,
Yet let him serve her till the day he's dead.
In truth, I praise not what the goose has said.
Even if she died, no other would I woo:
Until my death, to her I would be true.'   588

'Some joke!' then quacked the duck, 'Why, by my hat,
Should man swear love, and never have a chance?
What wit or reason can one find in that?
Who feeling gloomy joins a merry dance?

Why love a lady who repels romance?
Some quacking!' Thus the duck spoke loud and fair,
'God knows, there are more stars than just one pair!' 595

Then spoke the falcon: 'Low-class fellow, fie!
From off the dunghill came that speech all right!
The proper course of things escapes your eye!
You're struck by love as owls are by the light:
They're blinded by the day, and see by night.
Your breed is of so low a wretchedness
That what love is, you neither see nor guess.' 602

Then spoke the cuckoo, by his own caprice,
For birds that feed on worms, with this loud cry:
'As long as I can have my mate in peace,
Contend for ever if you like, say I.
Let all of them stay single till they die!
That's my advice, since they cannot agree.
No need to spell it out again, you see!' 609

'Yes, when the glutton's fully stuffed his paunch,'
The merlin said, 'the rest can then proceed!
You killer of the sparrow on the branch,
Who brought you up? You dismal slave of greed,
Stay single, you of worm-devouring breed!
No need for birds like you to spawn, I say:
Stay ignorant until the Judgement Day!' 616

'Now peace!' said Nature, 'I am mistress here!
Since I have pondered all you have to say –
And in effect agreement's nowhere near –
Attend my judgement in this case, I pray:
The formel eagle shall herself convey
Her choice; and whether you like it or demur,
At once the one she picks must partner her. 623

'For since by argument we can't agree
Who loves her best, just as the falcon said,

146

Then I shall please the formel, so that she
Shall have the one on whom her heart is set,
And one whose heart is fixed his bliss shall get.
Thus judge I, Nature, who can never lie;
From rank and special case I turn my eye.   630

'But as to counsel in a mating choice,
If I were Reason, certainly should I
To the royal eagle give my special voice,
For as the falcon best did amplify,
He is the noblest and of worth most high.
In pleasure I created him to excel,
And that should be enough for you as well.'   637

'My rightful lady, sovereign goddess Nature,'
In voice of awe the formel made reply,
'Exactly as each other earthly creature,
Ever under your rod of rule stand I,
And I shall be your own until I die.
So therefore grant the boon I ask of you,
And I shall tell you what I mean to do.'   644

'I grant it you,' said Nature. Straight away
The formel eagle made the following plea:
'Almighty Queen! For one year from today
I beg a respite to think privately,
And after that to give my verdict free.
I've no more words, for this is all that I
Can say, though you condemn me now to die: 651

'To serve Venus and Cupid I'll not stir
For yet a while, in any sort of way.'
'Now since it cannot otherwise occur,'
Said Nature, 'there is nothing more to say.
My wish is for these birds to fly away,
Each with his mate, and not stay longer here.'
And then she spoke to them as you shall hear.   658

'To you I speak, you eagles, I declare.
Be of good heart, and serve her well, all three;
A year is not so long for you to bear.
And each of you must suffer worthily,
And do his best for, God knows, she is free
From you for a year. Whatever then befall,
This interim is ordered for you all.'   665

And when they'd finished all that argument,
The goddess gave a mate to every bird
In full accord, and on their ways they went.
O Lord! with what delight and bliss they stirred!
For each with wings and arching neck then spurred
His partner in the deed of loving creature,
Thanking the while the noble goddess Nature.   672

But first, as was their custom year by year,
Some birds were picked to sing a sweet farewell,
A roundel as a parting song to cheer
And honour Nature and to please her well.
The tune was made in France, I truly tell;
The English words are such as you may find
In these next stanzas, which are in my mind: 679

'Now welcome, summer, with your sunshine soft!
The winter weather you have put to flight,
And driven off the season of black night.

Saint Valentine, who is so high aloft,
The little birds sing thus for your delight:
The winter weather you have put to flight,
And driven off the season of black night.

They have good cause for gladness oft and oft,
Since each one freshly has his partner bright;
They sing in bliss when they awake to light.
Now welcome, summer, with your sunshine soft!
The winter weather you have put to flight,
And driven off the season of black night!'   692

The Parliament of Birds

And with the shouting when the song was done
That those birds joyed in as they flew away,
I awoke, and other books had soon begun
To read. Indeed, I read my books all day,
And hope for sure some happy time I may
Read something to improve myself; therefore
I shall continue reading all the more.   699

The Legend of Good Women

INTRODUCTION TO
'THE LEGEND OF GOOD WOMEN'

This collection of legends was probably written in 1385–6, and the first version of the Prologue at about the same time. Of the two existing versions of the Prologue, called respectively 'F' and 'G' and usually printed side by side in editions of the poem, I have preferred the latter. In it, matter linking the poem decisively with Richard II's queen, Anne, who died in 1394 and was passionately lamented by the king, is altered. Norton Smith, in *Geoffrey Chaucer*, argues that the changes reduce the sense of design in the poem, but I find the G version, which is a late revision, more satisfying. Yet I do offer the sixteen lines from 'F' containing the beautiful harp compliment, which was presumably meant for Queen Anne (p. 162).

For the main love vision material in the Prologue, precedents existed in contemporary French poetry for the praise of the daisy, for the charge of heresy against Love, and of course for the appearance of the God of Love himself. In the stories that follow, for all but two Chaucer drew on Ovid; the exceptions are the tales of Cleopatra, whose history is twice told by Boccaccio, and of Dido, for whom his main source was the *Aeneid*, though he also drew on Ovid's *Heroides*.

Posterity has rated the Prologue high, chiefly on account of the magical praise of the daisy and the Chaucerian auto-biography, and the legends low, mainly because they are inferior to the tales told by Chaucer's pilgrims on the way to Canterbury. The legends suffer because their heroines are long-dead classical figures and 'heathens, all the lot' (l.299), instead of being English and rooted in a living society. Besides, many of them have been fully treated in more familiar works. In addition, there is no unifying device which brings each story into special focus in relation to its narrator – which is one of the distinguishing characteristics of *The Canterbury Tales*. The unifying device offered is the single theme of feminine steadfastness and masculine treachery as defined in Alcestis's final instruction to the poet (ll.470–79); which might tend to confine the potentiality of such a poet as Chaucer, and to encourage the writing of stories lacking in psychological subtlety, narrative complexity and suspense – if the prescription were closely followed. That is the evident literary penalty for having written at length about false Cressida in *Troilus and Criseyde*, to which this poem is a direct palinode.

To the Prologue first, then. For all the courtly conventions and lyrical engagement with Nature's beauties, human and floral, the central concern is the judgement of the poet, viewed autobiographically before and after his trial. He admits his dependence on books and his almost rueful acceptance of their 'old stories' as material for his poetry. Throughout the four poems in this book there is an unresolved tension, in the search for truth, between the authority of books and the experience of life. Chaucer cannot be blamed, it is suggested, for the instruction offered in ancient books which he retails.

When he is censured by the God of Love, that beautiful but frightening figure with glowing wings, holding two 'fiery darts', it is for publicizing the lore of Love as represented in *The Romance of the Rose*. That is the shock communication of the Prologue, which should alert us to the possibility that satire and self-parody exist among its St Valentine's Day outpourings. For if the God of Love regards *The Romance of the Rose* as 'all heresy' against his law (l.255), what of the conventional loyalties of the courtly poet, and what law does the God of Love recommend? Something like the synthesis offered at the end of 'The Parliament of Birds', perhaps? Whatever the answer, we must be sure of two things: the tap-root of courtly love poetry is scorned, and the stories Chaucer tells in carrying out the royal instruction make light of both courtly love values and Christian morality. They are, indeed, all about feminine constancy in love, and most of them are also about masculine perfidy; but sometimes the tone of the narration, and often the poet's final comment on a story, suggests that his tongue is in his cheek. For example, his attitude to Phyllis's letter (ll.2513–17) might bring to mind such a moment from the Prologue as that when Chaucer, self-indulgently retiring to his arbour for the night and its love-dream, orders his servants to scatter flowers on his bed (l.101).

The stories themselves express what D. S. Brewer in *Chaucer: The Critical Heritage 1385–1933*, vol.1, p.44) has called 'Gothic femininity', a quality he opposes to medieval priestly anti-feminism. Viewed from our age, which is adjusting to the achievements of the women's movement, 'Gothic femininity' in Chaucer presents women, albeit sympathetically, as people who can conceive no natural and desirable alternative or addition to their subservient role. Heroines in this poem exist for love of man alone; none can even think of either revenge or an alternative strategy. Perhaps they, and the long poem in which they figure, were dismissed when the poet conceived the Wife of Bath? It must be observed that, largely on account of the limited prescript imposed by Alcestis, even the initiatives some of them expressed in their original classical stories are denied them, and their spiritual energy and ambition are used exclusively to inflate the balloons of masculine egos. To take them one by one:

Cleopatra, who here makes her first appearance in English literature (and as one of Cupid's saints at that) is a noble queen who never murdered her dynastic rivals, never thought of betraying Antony to the beardless Caesar. She does take part in a fierce sea-battle, recounted in a boisterous alliterative style reminiscent of a different school of poets, but the whole point of her story is to hurry her to a death which demonstrates utter fidelity to the dead hero. Not content with embalming his body and filling his tomb with jewels, she applies no tiny asp to either of her royal breasts, but wholeheartedly leaps stark naked into a pit full of snakes.

Thisbe's name, like Cleopatra's, has been used by Shakespeare to elicit responses at variance with the old story. Chaucer's legend is a genuinely pretty tale of pathetic young love, frustrated initially by 'wretched jealous fathers two' and destroyed eventually by a roving lioness. Like Antony, Pyramus, the man in the case, was no heartless traitor, and the male chauvinist concluding point is that 'A woman can dare and do as well as he' (l.923).

Dido here receives her second Chaucerian genuflection in this book, and it is the main one. It draws heavily on Virgil, but the long passage in which Dido is described falling in love with Aeneas and heaping hospitality and love upon him is profoundly medieval in setting and detail. To begin with, all is selected for its focus on love: we are carried along on Dido's unreflecting passion until the moment (l.1254) of Chaucer's apostrophe to women on the perfidy of men. After that, the pathos of Dido's loss is mingled with the poet's affected boredom. This is the tale which first gave me the idea that Chaucer may have been writing particularly for a society of noble ladies: in it he first titillates romantic sensibility, and then relaxes into a condemnation of men beside which the suffering of the recently deserted heroine has become less interesting. It is a chemical emotional effect proper to the story-teller in an oral tradition: listening as a member of a group, one may, privately, wallow sensually in the body of the story, but as the end approaches, one is less exposed if the audience of which one is a member can be united in light humour.

In the legend of Hypsipyle, Chaucer approaches the knockabout style in which, in several of *The Canterbury Tales*, he rejoices in *fabliau*-type seduction. The tale starts loftily, with the island queen succouring the sea-battered heroes, Jason and Hercules; but soon (1520ff.) she falls to a conspiracy in which Hercules acts as pander, and one is reminded of the plotting of John and Aleyn, the two poor scholars in 'The Reeve's Tale' who lie with the Miller's wife and daughter.

The promiscuousness of Jason is further celebrated – indeed, this fourth legend has one hero, Jason, rather than two heroines – in the short account of his seduction and abandonment of Medea, whose titanic classical propensities for magic and revenge receive virtually no mention. Chaucer shows that he is writing with Ovid's *Heroides* at his elbow, but in every tale except that of Phyllis he resists the lengthy pathos of his Latin master's Epistles. More to the purpose is his short prologue, in which he inveighs against Jason as a fox-like chicken thief. To have this farmyard villain pleading in courtly style with mysterious heroines from classical legend, who then proceed to give him their worldly goods as well as their bodies, no doubt diverted Chaucer's noble audiences in a none too lofty manner.

The legend of Lucrece is a pretty one, prettier even than that of Thisbe; and both are delicate, unlike the legends of Hypsipyle and Medea. Chaucer is attached to the principle of variety, and knows that he can genuinely raise his audience, as with the Legend of Lucrece, as well as divert them with a courtly imitation of popular story-telling. With stories as short as these the suspense – what there is of it – is in the variety of the succession. Here the shamefast perfection of the heroine, inarticulate at her two terrible moments, the one of being raped and the other of committing suicide, contrasts with the brutal explicitness of Tarquin's crime. Nowhere else in this book is Venus's third power, the incitement to lust, as sharply evinced as in Tarquin's imaginings (ll.1745–74). After such real horror, Chaucer's audience would experience civilized amusement at the sainted lady's concern, as she fell dying, modestly to cover her naked feet and other parts (l.1859). The light and sententious ending is again appropriate to public performance.

With the Legend of Ariadne, Chaucer offers a comic sophistication on the theme of heroic love, as remote as can be imagined from the world of the Rape of Lucrece. Here, perhaps for the first time, we can see the wit that was to go into the Tale of Sir Thopas. The target, however, is not the English ballad romance, but the combined venerabilities of classical myth and medieval French and English homage to that myth. After a largely irrelevant preliminary about the siege of Megara and Scylla's treachery (see Notes), Chaucer explains the opening situation, and gives the game away at once by suggesting the core event of the story (ll.1956–8). With Theseus in prison waiting to be fed to the Minotaur, we meet the heroine and her sister on the walls above, mooning. Beneath them, an abutting privy gives them a connection with the sorrowing prisoner whose laments they overhear. There is some doubt about the word 'foreyne', but it does seem to mean 'privy'; which makes the moonlight conversation of Ariadne and Phaedra, on the walls above, pleasantly ridiculous. Next comes Phaedra's suggestion that the Minotaur's teeth can be gummed up and so made harmless if Theseus throws balls of tow into his gaping maw. Practical women, these ancient Cretans. So practical that when Theseus, learning of their determination to save his life, professes courtly humility and service, Ariadne at once proposes to him (l.2089), and suggests titles for herself and her sister when they arrive safely in Athens. Theseus replies, almost in burlesque style, that he had in fact been in love with her for years – though it is clear that they had never met before. The coincidences pile up, and Theseus's sudden preference for Phaedra, which makes him abandon Ariadne on Naxos, sees this martyr of love, practical to the last, tying her headscarf to a pole and waving it at Theseus's receding ship.

The next of Cupid's saints is Philomela, heroine of perhaps the grisliest of classical myths in which rape figures and, significantly for the mechanism of courtly love, the lady whose agony is represented whenever the nightingale sings. Chaucer's story seems designed for those who know the outcome, but this time, instead of giving away the ending, he first creates a wide pathos of family feeling, so that the rape and the cutting out of Philomela's tongue come as a strong shock. Her piteous cries are appeals to her father and sister, and thus more desolate. The humour is kept for the very end, and directed to abusing men for their cruelty. This legend and the next end with personal jokes in which the poet draws attention to himself.

Phyllis, the last saint but one in this Legendary, is another coastal queen who, like Dido and Hypsipyle, succours a storm-tossed philanderer. This is the tale in the telling of which Chaucer draws more fully on Ovid's *Heroides*: we have much of Phyllis's pathetic letter of censure on her faithless lover, though not the long pathos of the Ovidian scene of Demophon's departure. This letter, says Robert Worth Frank, Jr (*Chaucer and The Legend of Good Women*, p.153) is something of 'a handbook for philanderers', which would certainly amuse my hypothetical audience.

In the last legend, that of Hypermnestra, the heroine is bound by astrological predetermination and dream prophecy. The latter persuades her father that he must avoid assassination by a nephew; and the only way to do it is to make his daughter kill her husband in the bridal bed. The former gives her a character which makes it impossible for her to wield a knife in anger. The whole series of scenes, beginning with the dire interview between father and daughter, and ending with the heroine sitting in despair to await her father's vengeance because she is unable to run fast enough to accompany her fleeing husband, is intensely dramatic. A fierce tale, graphically and economically told.

In selecting from the source stories, Chaucer ignores features which are not to his pathetic or humorous purpose, and often improves the effect of the dénouement – the abandonment of, or the violence perpetrated on, his heroines – by first placing and characterizing his saint. Hypsipyle, 'a-pleasuring / And roaming on the cliffs beside the sea', and Lucrece in undress, weaving with her maids, come to mind. But Chaucer's constant theme, which appears again and again in the accounts of heartless seduction, is the gullibility of women: Dido, Hypsipyle, Medea, Ariadne and Phyllis all receive indirect censure for failing to see through beauty, rank and warrior glamour to the rottenness within the man. And I suspect that this emphasized joke would especially appeal to Chaucer's audience. 'The Legend of Good Women' is a teasing poem, the sophisticated variety of which should not be undervalued merely because greater work was to follow.

THE LEGEND OF GOOD WOMEN
OR, THE LEGENDARY OF
CUPID'S SAINTS*

Prologue

A thousand times have I heard people tell
That there is joy in heaven and grief in hell,
And I agree that that may well be so;
But all the same, there's something else I know:
There's no one living in this land, I say,
Who's been to hell or heaven and come away,
Or knows a thing except that he could quote
From something someone said, or even wrote!
No man can prove it by an actual test.
Yet God forbid! Men may the truth attest   10
Of many things without the proof of eye.
For people shouldn't think a thing a lie
Because no person saw it long ago.
A thing is just as real, and not less so,
Although it can't be seen by every man.
Some things, by God! escaped Saint Bernard's scan!*

   And so it is to books, in which we find
Those ancient things remaining in the mind,
And to their teaching in an antique style,
That we must give belief, and to the guile   20
With which they tell their well-attested stories
Of holiness, and realms, and triumph's glories,
Of love, of hate, of other subjects too,
Which at the moment I shan't list for you.
If ancient books were lost or ceased to be,
Then lost would be the key of memory.
So we should trust to what the old books say:
To prove the truth, there is no other way.

And as for me, although my wit is small,
I find that books most happily enthral;   30
That I so reverence them in my heart,
So trust their truth, so pleasure in their art,
That there is scarce a single joy I know
That can persuade me from my books to go,
Except, perhaps, upon a holy day,
Or else in the ecstatic time of May,
When all the little birds begin to sing,
And flowers start to blossom and to spring.
Farewell my study while the spring days last!
    Now as for spring, my liking is so cast   40
That, of all the meadow flowers in sight,
I most adore those flowers red and white
Which men call daisies in the region round.
To them I'm so affectionately bound,
As I declared before, in time of May,
That when I lie in bed there dawns no day
But has me up and walking on the lawn
To see these flowers spread towards the dawn
When sunrise brings the light with brilliant sheen,
The livelong day thus walking on the green.   50
And when the sun goes down towards the west,
It draws its petals in and shuts in rest
Until the morrow brings the morning light,
So greatly frightened is it of the night.
    This daisy, of all lovely blooms the flower,
Replete with virtue, honour's pretty dower,
And constant in its beauty and its hue,
Alike in winter as in summer new,
Its praises, if I could, I would distil;
But sad to say, it is beyond my skill!   60
For men before my time, I can be sworn,
Have reaped the fields and carried off the corn;
And I come after, gleaning here and there,
And am delighted if I find an ear,
A graceful word that they have left behind.
And if I chance to echo in my mind

What they sang freshly in authentic song,
I trust they will not think I've done them wrong,
Since what I write is done to praise the power
Of those who erstwhile served the leaf or flower.*   70
For be assured, I do not undertake
To attack the flower for the green leaf's sake,
Nor yet to set the flower against the leaf:
As if I'd set the corn against the sheaf!
I give sole love, or am averse, to neither;
I'm not specifically attached to either.
Who serves the flower or leaf I do not know.
That's not the purpose of my present throe,
Which is concerned with quite another span:
That of old tales, before such strife began.   80
    The reason that I advocate belief
In ancient books and reverence them in chief
Is this: men should believe authorities
Since in all other tests no firm proof lies.
I mean, before I leave you for elsewhere,
The naked text in English to declare
Of tales or exploits ancient authors told.
Believe them if you will: they're very old!

The 'F' text, in which Chaucer at first appears to favour the Flower against the Leaf, has this lovely passage instead of ll.69 – 80 above:

  ... Since what I write is honour to the power
  Of love, and in true service of the flower
  Whom I shall serve while I have wit or might.
  She is the brightness and the perfect light
  That in this dark world shows, and steers my course.
  The heart within my sad breast with such force
  Respects and loves you that of my true wit
  You are the mistress: I guide none of it.
  My words and deeds are so in your command
  That, as a harp obeys the player's hand,
  And sings according to its fingering,

So from my heart-strings you can always bring
What voice you please, to laugh or to complain.
Be ever my guide and Lady Sovereign!
To you as to my earthly god I cry
Both in this poem and when my woes I sigh.

*

When it was towards the very end of May,
And I had wandered all a summer's day   90
That verdant meadow that I told you of
The new-sprung daisies to admire with love,
And when the sun had sunk from south to west,
And shut up was the flower, and gone to rest
At gloom of night, at which she felt such dread.
Then homeward to my house I quickly sped;
And in a little arbour I possess,
New-benched with fresh-cut turves for tidiness,
I had my servants dress my couch for night;
To celebrate the summer's fresh delight,   100
I bade them scatter flowers on my bed.
When I had covered up my eyes and head,
I fell asleep within an hour or two.
I dreamed that I was on that lawn anew
And that I wandered in the selfsame way
To see the daisy as you've heard me say.
And all that lawn, it seemed to me, was fair,
With pretty flowers embroidered everywhere.
One speaks of gum's, or herb's, or tree's fine scent:
To no comparison would I consent.   110
Its perfume outdid other scents by far;*
In beauty it surpassed all flowers that are.
The earth had quite forgotten winter's dread,
Which stripped him naked, leaving him for dead,
And with his icy sword struck him with grief.
To that the temperate sun now brought relief
And freshly clothed the earth in green again.
  The little birds, in early summer's vein,
At least those who'd survived the noose and net,
Sang out defiance of him who'd so beset   120

163

Them all in winter, killing off their brood,
The cruel fowler, for it did them good
To sing of him, and in their song revile
The filthy churl who with his cunning guile
And avarice had tricked them wickedly.
This was their song: 'The fowler we defy!'
And on the branches some birds sang out clear
Their love songs, which were pure delight to hear,
Each one in praise and honour of a mate,
And blissful summer's start to celebrate*   130
Upon the branches fluttering aloft
In their delight among the blossoms soft.
They trilled out, 'Blessed be Saint Valentine!*   131
For on his day I choose you to be mine,
Which I shall not repent, my own heart's sweet!'
With that their beaks came gently in to meet,
Conveying honour and humble salutations,
And after that they had such celebrations
As are appropriate to love and nature,
And are performed indeed by every creature.
To hear their singing I was most intent
Because I dreamed I knew just what they meant.   140
   Presently a lark sang out above.
'I see,' she sang, 'the mighty God of Love.
Look where he comes! I see his wings outspread.'
And then I looked along the flowery mead
And watched him pacing, leading forth a queen
Attired in royal array, and all in green.
And on her hair she wore a golden net,
On top of which a crown of white was set
With many flowers. It's true what I write down:
For all the world, as daisies have a crown   150
Made up of many small white petals bright,
So she too had a crown of flowery white.
Of one piece only was this crown of white,
A single eastern pearl unflawed and bright,
Which made the white crown up above the green
Exactly like a daisy in its sheen,

Considering the golden net above.
    The garments of this mighty God of Love
Were silk, adorned all over with green boughs;
He had a rose-leaf garland on his brows,   160
Which held a host of lily-flowers in place.
I could not see the expression on his face
Because his countenance shone out so bright
Its gleaming brilliance amazed the sight;
A furlong off, he dazzled still my eye.
But in his hands at length I did espy
Two fiery darts, like coals both glowing red,
And angel-like his glowing wings he spread.
The God of Love is blind, or so men say,
But I thought he could see well every way,   170
Because he fixed on me the sternest look,
Which when I saw, my heart turned cold and shook.
And by the hand he held that noble queen,
Who wore a crown of white and robes of green,
And was so womanly, benign and meek
That though you travelled all this world to seek,
Not half her beauty would you ever find
In any creature of a natural kind.
And she was called Alcestis,* bright and fair;
I pray God may she prosper everywhere!   180
For if she'd not been present with her balm,
Then doubtless I'd have died in sheer alarm,
Helpless before his words and fierce look,
As I shall tell you later in my book.
    Behind the God of Love, upon that green,
Some ladies I observed, in all nineteen,*
Walking in royal robes with gentle tread,
And such a host of womankind they led,
I could not think that there had ever been
A third or fourth of those who now were seen   190
In all this wide created world since God
Constructed Adam from the earthly sod.
And every one of them was true in love.
    Whatever wonder this was token of,

The very moment that there came in sight
That flower I call the daisy fair and bright,
They suddenly all stopped instinctively
And went down on their knees most purposefully.
And then they all danced gently in a ring
Around this flower. I watched them dance and sing   200
In manner of a carole, and I heard
Their ballad and shall tell you every word:

Hide, Absalom, thy tresses gold and clear,*
   And Esther, lay thy gentle meekness down,
And Jonathan, conceal thy friendly cheer;
   Penelope, and Marcia, Cato's own,
   Make of your wifehood no comparison;
Isolde, Helen, hide your beauties' light:
Alcestis here bedims your lustre bright.

Thy lovely body, let it not appear,   210
   Lavinia; thou, Lucrece of Roman town;
Polyxena, who bought thy love so dear;
   Thou, Cleopatra, nobly passionate one;
   Hide all your faithful loves and your renown;
And Thisbe, whom love brought such pain and fright:
Alcestis here bedims your lustre bright.

Hero and Dido, Laodamia dear,
   And Phyllis, hanging for thy Demophon,
Thou Canacee, whose woes in thee appear;
   Hypsipyle, betrayed by Aeson's son,   220
   Boast not your faith in love, make no proud moan;
Ariadne, Hypermnestra, bear your plight:
Alcestis here bedims your lustre bright.

The singing of this ballad being done,
By order in a circle every one
Of all those ladies gentle and serene
Sat down upon the grass so soft and green.
First sat the God of Love, and next, this queen

Attired in crown of white and robes of green,
Then in due order others by degree   230
Of noble rank were seated courteously;
And not a word was spoken in that place
Within the radius of a furlong's space.
Upon a grassy slope close by I waited
To learn what these fine people contemplated,
As still as any stone, until at last
The God of Love his eyes upon me cast
And then demanded, 'Who's that over there?'
Which when I heard, I gave him answer fair,
Saying, 'My lord, it's I,' and going near,   240
Saluted him. 'What are you doing here,'
He asked, 'so bold and in my presence now?
For it were better a worm should come, I vow,
Before my eyes than you, I'd have you know.'
'If you please, my lord,' said I, 'why so?'
'Because,' said he, 'you're quite incapable.
My servants are all wise and honourable,
But you're among my deadly enemies,
And lie about my former devotees,
Misrepresenting them in your translation,   250
And stopping folk from making dedication
Of service to me. While to trust to me,
You can't deny, you say is lunacy.
To put it plainly, everybody knows
That by translating *The Romance of the Rose*,
Which is all heresy* against my law,
You've made wise people from my rule withdraw.
Your mind and reason, being somewhat cool,
Reckon a person is a perfect fool
Who loves intensely with a burning fire.   260
By that I see you're doddering in desire
Like ancient fools with failing spirits, who blame
The rest and don't know what is wrong with them.
Have you not put in English too the book
Of Troilus, whom Cressida forsook,
Thus demonstrating women's perfidy?

But all the same, this question answer me:
Why won't you write of women's uprightness
Now that you've written of their wickedness?
Was there no good material in your mind?   270
In all your books could you not somewhere find
A tale of women who were good and true?
By God, yes, sixty volumes old and new
Do you possess, all full of stories great
That Roman poets, and Greek as well, relate
Of various women, what sorts of life they had;
And ever a hundred good against one bad.
This God knows well, and so do scholars too
Who seek such histories, and find them true.
What say Valerius,* Livy,* Claudian?   280
What says Jerome against Jovinian?*
How pure were virgins and how true were wives,
How constant too were widows all their lives,
Jerome recounts, and not of just a few –
More like a hundred, that would be my view.
It's pitiful and makes the spirit sore
To read the woes which for their faith they bore,
For to their loves they were so wholly true
That rather than take on a lover new
They chose to die in various horrid ways,   290
And ended as each separate story says.
For some were burnt, some had their windpipes slit,
Some drowned because no sin would they commit;
But every one retained her maidenhead,
Or widow's vow, or troth with which she wed.
They did it not for love of holiness,
But love of purity and righteousness,
Lest men should mark them with a vicious blot;
Yet all of them were heathens, all the lot,
Who were so fearful of incurring shame.   300
These bygone women so preserved their name
That in this world I think you will not find
A single man who'd be as true and kind
As lowliest woman at that early date.

What does Ovid's famed *Epistle** state
Of faithful wives and all their doings, pray?
Or in *History's Mirror*, Vincent of Beauvais?*
All authors, Christians and pagans too,
The wide world over, write of such for you.
It doesn't need all day to put you right.   310
But yet what's wrong with you, that when you write,
You give the chaff of stories, not the corn?
By sainted Venus, from whom I was born,
Although you have renounced my law and creed,
As other old fools often have, take heed!
You shall repent, as shall be widely seen!'
    At once up spoke Alcestis, noblest queen,
Saying, 'God, the dues you owe to courtesy
Require you to attend to his reply
On all these points that you have put to him.   320
A god should not appear so cross and grim,
But should be stable in his deity,
With justice and true magnanimity.
His anger rightfully he cannot wreak
Until he's heard the other party speak.
Not all is true that you have heard complained;
The God of Love hears many a tale that's feigned.
For in your court is many a flatterer,
And many a strange accusing tattler,
Who in your ears will drum some ugly thing,   330
Born of hate or jealous imagining,
Just to enjoy with you some dalliance.
Envy – I pray God deal her all ill-chance! –
Is laundress in the royal court, I say,
For she will never leave, by night or day,
The house of Caesar. Dante made it plain:
Whoever leaves, the laundress will remain.
Perhaps this man has wrongly been accused,
So that in justice he should be excused.
Or else, my lord, the man is so precise   340
He makes translations with no thought of vice,
Just versifying what in books is there,

Of subject matter hardly being aware.
And so *The Rose* and *Cressida* he wrote
In innocence, of harm not taking note.
Or he was forced that pair of books to choose
By somebody, and did not dare refuse;
For he has written many books ere this.
He has not done as grievously amiss
In rendering new what ancient poets penned,   350
As if with malice and with foul intent
He'd written poems himself in Love's despite.
That's how a lord should think who cares for right,
And not be like the Lords of Lombardy,*
Who rule by wilful fit and tyranny.
For one who's naturally a lord or king
Should not be cruel and given to bullying
As is the excise-man, who does what harm he can;
But knowing his duty, he should treat the man
As liegeman, since he owes that loyalty   360
To all his people, and benignity,
And should attend to all their pleas with care,
Complaints, petitions, every law affair
When it's put up, for judgement in due course.
For this rule, Aristotle* is the source:
It is the duty of a king to make
And keep good law for every liegeman's sake.
Good kings have sworn to that their deepest vow
For many hundred winters up till now;
Sworn too to keep their aristocracy,   370
As it is right and wise that they should be
Enhanced and honoured, given favours dear,
For they are half-gods in this world down here.
For rich and poor alike this law is meant,
Although their state of life is different.
For poor folk everyone should feel compassion;
See how the lion behaves in gentle fashion!
For when a fly annoys or stings him, he
Wafts it away with tail quite easily;
His noble sentiments are set so high   380

He won't avenge himself upon a fly
As would a cur or beast of low-born taint.*
A lordly spirit ought to show restraint
And weigh up each event in equity
With due regard for noble dignity.
For Sire, it shows no prowess in a lord
To damn a man who's not allowed a word
In his defence. That is a foul abuse:
And even if he offers no excuse,
But pleads for mercy with a grieving heart,   390
And begs you, kneeling to you in his shirt,
To give your judgement as you deem it fit,
A god should briefly then consider it,
Weighing his honour and the person's crime.
And since there is no cause for death this time,
You shouldn't find it hard to show some grace:
Dismiss your rage and show a kindly face.
The man has served you with his poet's skill:
Your love-laws he has helped you to fulfil.
When he was young he propped up your estate: 400
I don't know if he's now a runagate.
But I know well, the things that he can write
Persuade unlearned folk to take delight
In serving you and honouring your name.
He wrote the book that's called *The House of Fame*,
The book of Blanche the Duchess' death no less,
The Parliament of Birds too, as I guess,
Arcite and Palamon of Thebes's love,*
A story very few have knowledge of,
And many hymns to you for holy days   410
As well, called ballads, roundels, virelays.*
Of other products of industriousness,
He has in prose translated Boethius,
The Miserable Engendering of Mankind,
Which in Pope Innocent the Third you find,
And Saint Cecilia's life with all its woe:
And he translated, long long years ago,
Origen's homily on the Magdalen.*

He now deserves less punishment and pain,
Because he's written so many a lovely thing.   420
   Now, as you are a god and mighty king,
I, your Alcestis, sometime Queen of Thrace,
Ask on this man's behalf that in pure grace
You'll never do him harm in any way;
And he shall swear to you without delay
Never to be at fault as you describe;
And he shall write, as you should now prescribe,
Of women who loved truly all their lives,
What kind you will, of virgins, widows, wives,
To advance your cause, not smirch it, as in those   430
Stories he wrote of Cressida and the Rose.'
   The God of Love made answer straight away:
'My Lady, it is many and many a day
Since first I found you charitable and true,
So clearly so that since the world was new
I never found a better one than you.
And so to keep my state with honour due,
I will not, cannot, frown on your request.
He's yours, to do with him as you think best.
You may forgive, without a moment's pause,   440
For if you make a gift, or bless his cause,
And do it quickly, you'll be thanked the more.
Give judgement then what he must do therefore.
Go thank my Lady now!' he said to me.
   I rose, then settled down upon my knee
And humbly said, 'My Lady, God above
Repay you, since you've made the God of Love
Remove his anger from me and forgive!
Now grant with grace that I may so long live
As to be sure what person you may be,   450
Who helped me thus and put such trust in me.
Yet truly I believe that in this case
I have no guilt, and did Love no disgrace,
Because an honest man, I firmly plead,
Takes no part in a robber's wicked deed.
And no true lover ought to give me blame

Because I speak a faithless lover's shame.
They rather ought to give me their support
Because of Cressida I wrote the thought
My author had, as also of *The Rose*.   460
It was my wish completely, as God knows,
To further faith in love and cherish it,
And warn against betrayal and deceit
With my examples; that was what I meant.'*
    And she replied, 'Stop all that argument,
For Love won't have such plea and counter-plea
Of right and wrong; take that at once from me!
You've won your favour; closely hold thereto.
Now I will say what penance you must do
For your misdeed. Attend my judgement here: 470
During your lifetime, you shall year by year
Spend most part of your time in writing stories
Extolling all the legendary glories
Of virtuous women – virgins, honest wives –
Who kept their faith in loving all their lives;
And tell of traitors who were false to them
And made of all their lives a stratagem
To see how many women they could shame:
For in your world that's counted as a game.
Though love is not the thing on which you're bent,*   480
Speak well of it: that is your punishment.
And to the God of Love I shall so pray
That he shall charge his men in every way
To help you on, your labour to repay.
Your penance is but light; now go your way!'
    The God of Love then smiled at that and said,
'Can you tell me, is she wife or maid,
Or queen or countess? Of what rank is she
Who gave you penance of such small degree,
When you deserved more painfully to smart?   490
But pity quickly flows in gentle heart.
You can see that; she makes known who she is.'
And I replied, 'No, lord. May I have bliss,
But all I know of her is that she's good.'

'That story's true all right, and by my hood,'
Said Love, 'If you've a notion to be wise,
You'd better know it well, that's my advice.
Do you not have the book, in your big chest,
Of Queen Alcestis, full of virtues blest,
Who changed into a daisy, the day's eye,*   500
Who took her husband's place and chose to die,
And so instead of him to go to hell;
Whom Hercules brought out from there to dwell
On earth again, by God, and live in bliss?'
And I replied to him and answered, 'Yes,
I recognize her now. And is this sshe,
The daisy Alcestis, heart's felicity?
I deeply feel the goodness of this wife,
Who after death, as well as in her life,
Redoubled her renown with her largess.   510
She well repays the love that I profess
For her own flower. Small wonder that high Jove
Should set her as a star in heaven above
For all her virtues, as writes Agathon.*
Her white crown proves the fact to everyone;
For just as many virtues does she own
As there are little flowers in her crown.
In honour of her, to keep her memory,
The daisy flower was made by Cybele,*
As men may see, with white crown on her head,   520
To which Mars gave, by God, a touch of red
Instead of rubies, set amongst the white.'

At this, the Queen in shyness blushed a mite
At being praised so highly to her face.
Said Love then, 'Negligence has brought disgrace
On you for writing of inconstancy
In women, since you know their purity
By proof, as well as truth in old tales borne.
Ignore the chaff and celebrate the corn.
Tell Alcestis' story, I suggest;   530
Leave Cressida alone to sleep and rest.
For of Alcestis should your writing be;

Perfection's calendar, you know, is she.
She taught what perfect love should always do,
And chiefly what in wifely love is due,
With all the limits that a wife should keep.
Till now your tiny wit was fast asleep.
But now I order you, upon your life,
To write the legend of this perfect wife,
First writing others of a lesser brand;   540
And now farewell! For that's my last command.
At Cleopatra you should now begin,
And go from there; that way my love you'll win.'
With that, I awoke from sleep to shining day,
And started on my Legend straight away.

I

The Legend of Cleopatra, Queen of Egypt, Martyr

After the death of Ptolemy the King,*   580
Who had all Egypt in his governing,
His consort Cleopatra reigned as queen
Until it chanced, as history has seen,
That out of Rome a senator was sent
To conquer kingdoms and win settlement
Of honour for Rome, it being their practice then
To win the fealty of all earthly men,
And truth to tell, Mark Antony was his name.
It happened Fortune owed him grievous shame
So that he fell from high prosperity,   590
A rebel to the Roman polity.
And worse dishonour, Caesar's sister fair
He falsely abandoned, she being unaware,
And wanted at all costs another wife;
Thus he with Rome and Caesar fell to strife.
Yet all the same in truth this senator
Was valiant and a noble warrior
Whose death was a most dolorous event.
The love that filled him was so vehement,
He was so trapped in snares, in passion hurled,   600

By love for Cleopatra that the world
He valued not at all. Indeed it seemed
The only thing his moral sense esteemed
Was serving Cleopatra with his love.
Regardless of his life, in war he strove
To make defence of her and of her rights.
This noble queen adored this best of knights
For his deserving and his chivalry;
And certainly, unless the histories lie,
He was in person and in worthiness,   610
Discretion, courage and illustriousness,
Of noble living men the nonpareil;
And she was lovely as a rose in May.
And since things said are best in shortest measure,
She married him and had him at her pleasure.
For me, whose undertaking is to tell
So many stories and to tell them well,
Reporting of the wedding and the feast
Would take too long; when I should most, not least,
Report affairs of great effect and charge;   620
For men may overload a ship or barge.
So straight to the effect I now shall skip,
And all the minor things I shall let slip.
Octavian,* being furious at this deed,
Amassed an army which he meant to lead
To Antony's destruction utterly.
With Romans lion-cruel and hardy, he
Took ship, and thus I leave them as they sail.
Antony, aware, determined not to fail
To meet the Romans, could he find a way,   630
Made plans, and then he and his wife one day,
Delaying no longer, massed their mighty host,
Took ship with them and sailed along the coast,
And there the two fleets met.* With trumpet blasts
The shouts and firing starts, while each side casts
To get the sun behind its own attack.
The missile flies with fearful din and crack;
The fleets together grind in fierce clash

And down come balls of stone in crushing crash.
In goes the grapnel with its clutching crooks,   640
And, raking ropes and sheets, go shearing-hooks.
A fellow fetches blows with battle-axe
At one who round the mast flees the attacks,
Then out again, and heaves him overboard.
One stabs with spear, and one with point of sword;
One tears the sail with hooks as if with scythe.
One brings a cup and bids his mates be blithe,
Pours peas to make the hatches slippery,
Takes quicklime too to blind the enemy;
And thus the dragged-out day of fight they spend,   650
Till at the last, as all things have their end,
Mark Antony takes flight, a beaten man,
And all his forces flee as best they can.

The Queen flies too with all her purple sail
Before the blows, which beat as thick as hail;
No wonder! It was far too much to bear.
When Antony saw that misfortune there,
'Alas the day that I was born!' he said,
'From this day forth my honour's lost and dead!'
Despair unhinged his mind upon that word,   660
And through his noble heart he thrust his sword
Before he'd gone a footstep from the place.
His wife, who could not win from Caesar grace,
To Egypt fled in terror and distress.
Now listen, men who speak of tenderness,
Fellows who falsely promise, swearing blind
They'll die if their beloved proves unkind,
Just hear what sort of truth woman can show!
This wretched Cleopatra felt such woe
No tongue on earth could tell her mighty sorrow.   670
She did not pause, but swiftly on the morrow
Told subtle craftsmen to erect a shrine
With all the rubies and the jewels fine
In Egypt of which they could find supplies,
And filled the shrine with various kinds of spice
Which to embalm the body would combine,

Then fetched the corpse and shut it in the shrine.
And next the shrine she had dug out a grave,
And all the serpents that she chanced to have
She had put in that grave, and then she said,   680
'Now Love, whom my lamenting heart obeyed
So utterly that from that blissful time
I freely swore to keep your rule sublime –
Or Antony's, I mean, my noble knight –
I'd never waking, morning, noon or night
Allow you from my feeling, thinking heart,
For weal or woe, or song or dance, to part!
I swore then to myself that, weal or woe,
Exactly as you did, then I would so,
As fully as my powers could sustain,   690
Provided that my wifehood got no stain –
Yes, whether it would bring me life or death –
A covenant which, while I can draw breath,
I shall fulfil: and it shall well be seen,
There never was to love a truer queen.'
Full-hearted thus, she leapt into the pit*
Naked among the snakes that dwelt in it,
Desiring there to have her burial.
The serpents came to sting her one and all,
And she received her death with joyful cheer   700
For love of Antony, to her so dear.
I tell the truth, this is no yarn or fable.
Until I find a man so true and stable,
Who will for love his death so freely take,
I pray to God our heads may never ache!   AMEN

II

The Legend of Babylonian Thisbe. Martyr

Once upon a time in Babylon
Where Queen Semiramis* had had the town
Surrounded with a moat and walled about –
High walls with splendid well-baked tiles, no doubt –
There were residing in the noble town   710

Two princely lords of excellent renown,
Who lived so near each other on a green
That nothing but a stone wall lay between,
Of city boundaries the usual one.
And truth to tell, the one lord had a son,
In all that land one of the manliest.
The other had a daughter, loveliest
Of all those eastward dwelling in the place.
The name of each grew in the other's grace
Through gossips from the neighbourhood about,   720
For in that foreign land, without a doubt,
Virgins were strictly kept with jealousy
Lest they committed some loose levity.
The youthful bachelor's name was Pyramus,
The girl's was Thisbe, Ovid tells it thus.
Their reputations by report so throve
That as they grew in age they grew in love.
And truly, since their ages tallied quite,
Marriage between them would have been just right,
But that neither father would assent;   730
Yet both so burned with passion violent,
No friend of theirs could mitigate its force.
And secretly their true love took its course
And both of them expressed their strong desire.
'Cover the coal, and hotter grows the fire.'
And 'Ten times madder is forbidden love.'
A crack from top to base foundation clove
The wall which stood between these lovers two:
It had been so of old since it was new.
So narrow was this fissure in the wall,   740
So tiny, it could scarce be seen at all.
But is there anything Love can't espy?
These two young lovers – and I do not lie –
Were first to find that narrow little cleft.
And with a sound as soft as any shrift,
Their words of love were whispered through the wall,
And as they stood there, they went over all
Their sad lament of love, and all their woe,

Whenever it was safe to whisper so.
Upon the one side of the wall stood he,   750
And on the other side stood fair Thisbe,
Each there the other's sweet words to receive.
And in this way their guardian they'd deceive,
And every day that ancient wall they'd threaten,
And wish to God that it could be down beaten.
Thus would they speak, 'Alas, you wicked wall!
Your spiteful envy robs us of our all.
Why don't you cleave apart or break in two?
Or at the least, if that won't pleasure you,
You might just once allow us two to meet,   760
Just once to have the bliss of kissing sweet.
We'd then be cured of all our fatal woe.
But yet it is to you that we both owe
A debt because you suffer all the time
Our words to travel through your stone and lime;
And so we should be satisfied with you.'
And when their useless words were spoken through,
They'd kiss that cold unyielding wall of stone
And take their leave, and then they would be gone.
And this was chiefly in the eventide   770
Or early morning, lest it be espied.
They did the same a long time, till at length,
One day when Phoebus* brightly shone in strength –
Aurora* with her kindling morning gleams
Had dried the wet grass soaked in dewy streams –
Beside the crack as they were wont to do,
First Pyramus arrived, then Thisbe too,
And pledged their word with utmost faith that they
Would both of them that evening steal away,
Deceiving all their guardians as they went,   780
And leave the city, after which they meant,
The country fields being spacious, broad and wide,
At an appointed time to meet outside
At one fixed place, which they agreed should be
At Ninus'* kingly tomb beneath a tree –
For those who worshipped idols, so I've heard,

The pagans, used in fields to be interred –
And by this mausoleum was a well.
The covenant between them – and I tell
The story briefly – was compacted fast.   790
So long the sunshine seemed to them to last,
The sun would never set beneath the ocean.
   This Thisbe loved with such intense emotion,
And longed so much her Pyramus to see
That, when she saw that it was time to flee,
She stole away at night-time from her place
Disguised, a wimple covering her face.
To keep her promise she forsook her friends;
And it is pitiful that woman tends,
Alas! when she is under true love's spell,   800
To trust a man before she knows him well.
So to the tree she went at speedy pace,
Love making her determined in this case,
And then sat down and waited by the well.
Alas! A lioness most fierce and fell
Came from the wood at speed without delay,
Maw dripping blood from slaughtering her prey,
To drink from the well beside which Thisbe sat.
As soon as Thisbe was aware of that –
The moonlight made her see it fully clear –   810
She leapt up, heart benumbed with dread and fear,
And dashed into a cave in utter fright,
Dropping her wimple in her headlong flight
Regardless, being with terror so hard struck,
And glad that she'd escaped with so much luck.
She cowered in the darkness, very still,
And when the lioness had drunk her fill,
About the well she stalked and prowled around,
And straight away the maiden's wimple found,
And ripped and tore it in her bloody maw.   820
That done, she did not linger any more,
But to the forest once more took her way.
   At last came Pyramus with some delay,
For all too long at home, alas! stayed he.

The moon was shining; he could clearly see,
And on the path, as he was striding fast,
His searching look was always downward cast.
So looking down, there in the sand he saw
The spaced-out imprints of a lion's paw;
And suddenly he shuddered and grew pale.   830
His hair on end, he followed on the trail
And, finding there the wimple, ripped and torn,
He cried, 'Alas the day that I was born!
This single night shall both we lovers die!
Ask mercy of my Thisbe, how can I,
When I'm the one who slaughtered you, alas?
Through my request your death has come to pass.
Alas! To bid a woman go by night
Where dreadful dangers lurk to do her spite!
And I so slow I was not here – what shame! –   840
At least a furlong's length before you came.
Whatever lion prowls this wood, at least
My body he must tear! Whatever beast
Roams savage here must gnaw my heart, say I!'
He seized the wimple with a dreadful cry,
And kept on kissing it, and wept full sore,
Saying, 'Wimple, alas! I long for nothing more
Except that you should feel the blood of me
As you have felt the bleeding of Thisbe!'
Which said, right through his heart he thrust his sword.   850
Out of the wound the blood in wide streams poured,
Like water when a conduit-pipe has burst.

  Now Thisbe, knowing not of this at first,
But sitting terror-stricken, reasoned thus:
'If it should chance that my own Pyramus
Came here to seek me, and then did not find,
He'd think me faithless to him, even unkind.'
So she emerged at once to seek him out,
With heart and eyesight casting all about.
'I'll tell him how I feared the lioness,'   860
She thought, 'And everything I did, no less.'
And finally her loved one there she found,

Hammering with his heels upon the ground,
All bloody, which made her swiftly backwards start.
Like waves at sea then heaved her beating heart
And, pale as box-tree leaves, she came to see
And recognize her lover instantly,
Her Pyramus, her own heart's truest dear.
Who could describe the desperate deadly cheer
Of Thisbe then, and how she tore her hair,   870
And gave herself to torment and despair?
Ah, how she swooned and lay upon the ground,
And how she wept with tears that filled his wound!
How mingled she his blood with her complaint
By using it to daub herself, like paint!
How she embraced the dying corpse, alas!
This woeful Thisbe, come to such a pass!
And how she kissed his frosty mouth so cold!
'Who has done this? And who has been so bold
And killed my love? O speak, my Pyramus!   880
I am your Thisbe, calling on you thus.'
And thereupon she lifted up his head.

   This wretched man, who was not fully dead,
On hearing her the name of Thisbe cry,
Raised up to her his heavy, deathly eye,
Then let it fall, and yielded up the ghost.
Without a cry or moan Thisbe arose;
She saw her wimple, saw his empty sheath:
Saw too his sword, the sword which gave him death:
And then spoke thus: 'My grieving hand,' said she,   890
'Is strong enough to do the deed for me.
For love will give me strength and ruthlessness
To make a wound that's deep enough, I guess.
I'll follow you in death, and I shall be
Both cause and fellow of your death,' said she.
'Though only death could part us utterly,
You shall not even so escape from me,
For as you can't leave death, then I'll come too,
And in your death I shall companion you.
And now, you wretched jealous fathers two,   900

We who were once your children beg of you
That we, when you put further envy by,
May in a single grave together lie,
Since love has brought us to this piteous end.
May the just God to all true lovers send,
If they are faithful, more prosperity
Than ever came to Pyramus and me!
And may no lady thoughtlessly be sent
As I was to endure such accident.
Yet God forbid but that a woman can   910
Be just as true in loving as a man:
And as for me, I'll blazon it abroad.'
So saying, she at once took up his sword
Still hot with her love's heart-blood, as I say,
And thrust it through her own heart straight away.
And thus are Pyramus and Thisbe gone.
Men true in love I find but few or none
In all my books, except this Pyramus.
And that is why I've spoken of him thus.
For it is gratifying to us men to find   920
A man whose love is faithful, true and kind.
But here you see, great lover though he be,
A woman can dare and do as well as he.

III

The Legend of Dido, Queen of Carthage, Martyr

Glory and honour, Virgil the Mantuan,
Be to your name! I shall as best I can
Follow your lamp which lit up ere I came
Aeneas forswearing Dido, and their fame,
And take from Ovid and the *Aeneid*
The gist and great effects of what they did.
When Sinon with his wily Greek construction*   930
Caused Troy to fall and end in great destruction
By offering to Minerva* in pretence
A horse, and many Trojans perished hence;
When there'd appeared the ghost of Hector bold,

And fire so fierce it could not be controlled
Had burned down all of Troy it could devour,
Including Ilium, its chiefest tower;
And all that land was ravaged and brought low,
With Priam its king cut down and lost in woe;
Aeneas then was charged to flee the land   940
By Venus, so he grasped in his right hand
His son Ascanius,* and with him too,
Upon his back, his ancient father who
Was called Anchises; so he fled away,
But lost his wife Creusa by the way.
Much sorrow in his grieving mind had he
Till he could find and lead his company.
But at the last, when he had found his men,
He marshalled them in readiness, and then
He led them swiftly on towards the sea,   950
And all of them set sail for Italy,
The land where he'd fulfil his destiny.
Concerning his adventures on the sea,
To tell them here would be of no avail,
Since they don't fit the purpose of my tale.
But I shall stick, as I have now begun,
To his and Dido's story till it's done.

  So long he sailed upon the salty sea
That finally to Libya's coast came he
With only seven ships in his command;
And glad was he to hurry to the land,   960
Being shaken by the tempest, I declare.
He took possession of the harbour there,
And having with him in his knightly troop
Achates,* him he picked from all the group
To be his partner and spy out the land.
He took no other warriors from his band.
So lord and henchman left their ships to ride
At anchor and went forth without a guide.
They walked a long time in that desert bare,   970
And then at length they met a huntress there.
A bow in hand and arrows too had she;

Her skirt was short, cut close above the knee.
And yet she truly was the fairest creature
That ever had been made in mortal nature.
She, Lord Aeneas and Achates meeting,
Addressed them both as follows in her greeting:
'Have you, while ranging wide across the land,
Seen any of my sisters close at hand
With skirts tucked up and bow and arrow-case,   980
With boar or other quarry of the chase
That they have slaughtered in this forest wide?'
'No, truly, Lady,' then Aeneas replied,
'But with such beauty, so it seems to me,
An earthly woman you could never be;
For you are Phoebus' sister, so I guess,
And if in very truth you're a goddess,
Have mercy on our travail and our woe.'
She said, 'No goddess I, I'd have you know;
For girls go walking forth in this fair land   990
Like this, with bow and arrows in the hand.
You're now in Libya's kingdom, the demesne
Of Dido, who is lady here and Queen.'
She briefly told him all the circumstance
Of Dido's coming and her governance,
Concerning which I do not wish to rhyme.
It's pointless: it would be a waste of time.
The point is simply this: it was no other
Who spoke to him but Venus, his own mother.
She bade him go to Carthage that same day,   1000
And having told him, vanished clean away.
I'd copy Virgil word for word in style
Except that it would take too long a while.

    This noble queen called Dido, formerly
Sichaeus'* wife, whose beauty all might see
Was brighter than the beauty of the sun,
The founding of noble Carthage had begun.
Her rule there was so lofty and so good
That she was judged the flower of queenlihood
For noble grace, largess and elegance: 1010

Happy the man who looked upon her once!
By kings and lords she was so much desired
That all the world was by her beauty fired:
She stood most high in everybody's grace.
   Now when Aeneas had come into the place,
With unobtrusive stealth he made his way
Towards the town's chief temple where, I say,
Queen Dido was devotedly at prayer.
When he had entered that huge temple there,   1020
I cannot say if it be possible,
But Venus made him quite invisible –
I do not lie: it says it in the book.
When in this temple there they came to look,
Aeneas and Achates studied all
And found depicted there upon a wall
The ruin of Troy and all the land beside.
'Alas that I was born!' Aeneas sighed,
'Throughout the whole wide world they know our shame,
Which lurid paintings everywhere proclaim.
We who once lived in high prosperity   1030
Are now dishonoured, and to such degree
That to prolong my life I do not care!'
Upon which word he burst out weeping there
As pitifully as ever could be seen.
That ardent lady, Carthage city's Queen,
Stood in the temple in her royal gear.
So sumptuous and so fair did she appear,
So young, so vital, eyes a-glint with mirth,
That should our God, creator of heaven and earth,
Desire a love, for beauty and worthiness   1040
And womanliness and truth and seemliness,
Whom should he choose but that sweet lady bright?
For him no woman else could be so right.
Fortune, who keeps the world in governance,
Now suddenly brought in a lucky chance.
No luckier chance was ever so designed,
For all the company Aeneas had left behind,
Which in the tempest he had counted lost,

Had landed near the city on the coast.
Amongst the greatest of his lords were some   1050
Who by good luck had to the city come,
And to that very temple, there to speak
To Dido, and her gracious succour seek,
So justly famous was her kind largess.
And when they'd told the tale of their distress,
The tempest and the woes through which they'd been,
Aeneas came and stood before the Queen
And openly made known that it was he.
Who then rejoiced but all his company
Who'd found their lord and governor once more?   1060
The honour that they did him, Dido saw,
And having often heard Aeneas' fame,
She felt her heart with pity and grief a-flame
That ever such a noble man as he
Should be cut off from rule so cruelly.
She looked, and saw that he was like a knight,
A well-endowed and stalwart man of might,
The very pattern of nobility.
He framed his lofty utterance graciously,
Expressing well the splendour of his face,   1070
His strength of bone, his muscles' shapely grace.
For, being Venus' son, he was so fair
No man could look one half as fine, I swear;
He seemed to be a lord of sovereign kind.
And since he was a stranger, she inclined
Still more to like him, such was God's behest:
For some, what's new is often loved the best.
Her heart was struck with pity for his woe,
And with that pity, love came too; and so
Her sweet compassion and her graciousness   1080
Worked to refresh him in his dire distress.
She said how desolate in truth she was
For all his dangers past and heavy loss,
Addressing him with words of friendly cheer
And speaking kindly, as you now may hear:
'Are you not Venus and Anchises' son?

In truth, all courtesies that may be done,
All help and honour I can give, you'll have.
Your ships and all your company I'll save.'
And many a gentle word she gave him then,   1090
And sent out messengers from her own men
To find his ships, beginning that same day,
And victual them in full without delay.
First sending to the ships full many a beast,
With wine in barrels to make up the feast,
Straight to her royal palace did she stride,
Keeping Aeneas always at her side.
Their banquet there, what need have I to tell?
He never was delighted half as well.
Such dainties were there and such luxury,   1100
Such playing instruments, such songs of glee,
And many a loving look and quaint device.
Indeed Aeneas had come to Paradise
Out of the gulf of hell, and thus in joy
Looked back on his estate and life in Troy.

    Aeneas was led, the banquet being done,
To ballrooms full of hangings nobly spun,
With sumptuous couches, brilliant ornament,
Where he and Dido settled in content
With wine and spices shared in sweet delight,   1110
Until they led him to his room at night
With all his band, to take his rest at ease;
And all could do whatever most might please.
No well-caparisoned and bridled charger,
No easy-ridden palfrey small or larger,
No stallion snorting for the tournament,
No jewel with inlaid stones as ornament,
No loaded sacks of gold heavy and bright,
No crimson ruby shining out by night,
No noble heron-hunting falcon found,   1120
No boarhound, stag- or deer- or other hound,
No golden cup filled with florins new-chased,
That in the land of Libya could be traced,
But Dido had it to Aeneas sent;

And all was paid whatever he had spent.
And so her guests called this queen honourable
And in her largess unsurpassable.
Aeneas sent Achates, on his side,
Aboard his ship, it cannot be denied,
To fetch his son, and many sumptuous things,   1130
Clothes, sceptres, brooches, also many rings,
Some for himself to wear and some for her
Who'd made him gifts of noble character,
And tell his son to make the presentation
By taking to the Queen his own donation.
Achates soon came back, and full of joy
Aeneas was to see once more his boy,
His little son, the Prince Ascanius.
But yet our author makes it known to us
That Cupid, he who is the God of Love,   1140
Being asked to by his mother high above,
Assumed the likeness of the little child
So that the noble Queen might be beguiled
And love Aeneas: be that as it may,
I do not care what those old writings say.
The truth is that the Queen made mighty fuss,
A wonder to hear, of young Ascanius,
And for the presents that his father sent
She thanked him often with warm compliment.

    Thus was the Queen delighting in full joy   1150
With all those lively new-met folk from Troy.
She soon requested bold Aeneas to tell
His knightly deeds and what at Troy befell,
And all day long that pair most eagerly
Delighted in their talk and revelry,
From which activities grew such a fire
That Dido in the bliss of her desire
To dally with Aeneas, her new-come guest,
Lost all her colour and health in her unrest.

    Now to the result, the consequence of all   1160
When I have told the tale, as tell I shall.
I start like this: it happened one fine night

Just as the moon was throwing out its light,
This noble queen into her bedroom went,
And sighed and gave herself to languishment,
Sleepless and starting, tossing to and fro
As lovers do – at least I've heard it's so.
Eventually she told her sister Anne
And with heartfelt lamentings thus began:
'Dear sister, tell me what that thing might be   1170
That terrifies me in my dreams?' asked she.
'This Trojan newcomer so fills my mind,
Because he seems so shapely and refined,
And therefore like to prove a manly knight,
Achieving what is virtuous and right,
That in his hands lies all my love and life.
Have you not heard him tell his woes and strife?
Now truly, Anne, provided you agree,
Married to him I simply long to be.
This is reality, I can't deny: 1180
He has the power to make me live or die.'
Her sister Anne, advising for the best,
Declared that she by no means acquiesced;
And thereon followed such a long debate,
Until I ended it you couldn't wait.
But in the end Anne's point could not be gained:
Love must love on; it cannot be restrained.

   The dayspring being risen from the sea,
This amorous queen enjoined her men to see
To hunting nets and spears both broad and keen.   1190
A-hunting then would go this fresh young queen,
So sharp was her delightful languishment;
And so to horse her lively people went.
Into the courtyards all the hounds were brought,
And on their horses swift as any thought
Her youthful knights were waiting everywhere,
And crowds of ladies watched their menfolk there.
Upon a stalwart palfrey, paper-white,
Its saddle red, embroidered with delight,
With heavy bars of gold embossed, behold   1200

Queen Dido sitting, draped in jewels and gold,
As lovely as the sweetly shining morrow
That rescues sufferers from nights of sorrow.
Upon a charger mettlesome as fire –
You'd ride and turn him with a bit of wire –
Aeneas sat, like Phoebus I should say,
His garments shone in such a brilliant way.
The foamy bridle with the bit of gold
He managed well, and thus his mount controlled.
And so I leave this noble queen to ride   1210
Out hunting with the Trojan at her side.

   Right soon a herd of stags came into view
And then, 'Hey, on! Spur faster! View halloo!
Why won't a lion or a bear appear,
That I might face and have him with this spear?'
So cried the young men, moving in to kill
The wild beasts, and take them at their will.
Amidst all this heaven made a rumbling noise;
The thunder roared with terrifying voice;
Down came the rain with sleet and hail, so fast,   1220
With heaven-fire too, the hunt-folk were aghast.
The noble queen and all her company,
Each and every one, were glad to flee.
Queen Dido, from the storm intent to save
Herself, escaped into a little cave,
And this Aeneas also went with her.
What others went with them I am not sure;
Our author does not mention anyone.
And here the mighty passion was begun
Between these two; yes, here was the first morrow 1230
Of all their bliss, and start of all their sorrow.
For here it was Aeneas knelt down low,
Unlocked his heart and told her all his woe,
So swearing that to her he would be true,
Come weal or woe, nor leave for someone new,
Pleading as faithless lovers always feign,
That luckless Dido pitied all his pain,

Took him for husband and became his wife
For evermore, as long as they had life.
And after that, the tempest being spent,   1240
The two emerged in joy and homewards went.

   At once foul Rumour rose and made it known
That Dido and Aeneas had gone alone
Into the cave. What people thought, they averred,
And when the King, whose name was Iarbas,* heard,
Seeing that he had loved her all his life
And wooed her so that she would be his wife,
He grieved so sadly, with such wretched cheer,
That truly it was pitiful to hear.
But in Love's wars it always happens so   1250
That one man's laughter brings another's woe.
Aeneas now laughs, possessing much more joy
And fortune than he ever did in Troy.

   O luckless women full of innocence,
Pity and truth and sweet benevolence,
What makes you trust men's declarations so?
Why waste your pity on their seeming woe
When such examples are before your eyes
Of men forsworn, of lovers telling lies?
Where saw you one who never was unkind,   1260
Nor left his love, nor harmed her, nor maligned
Nor plundered her, nor bragged about his deed?
You see such things, and also you may read.
Be warned now by this well-bred warrior,
This Trojan with such skill in pleasing her,
Who puts on faith and deep humility,
Is so refined, observes such secrecy,
Performs love's duties with obedience,
And squires her at the feast and in the dance,
At temple-going, and home again at night,   1270
And fasts until his lady comes in sight,
And bears I know not what devices on
His shield to honour her; composes songs,
And jousts; with arms in fight does many things,

193

Sends letters to her, tokens, presents, rings;
Just listen how he serves his Lady dear!
When he was starving, so that death was near
From hunger or from peril on the sea,
From homeland fled a hapless refugee,
And all his men by tempest overwhelmed,   1280
She made him gift of body and of realm
At his command, although she might have been
Of other lands, not only Carthage, Queen,
And lived in ample joy; what would you more?
Aeneas, who such fervent promise swore,
Soon tires of playing the devoted lover;
His earnest passion very soon blows over.
He secretly prepares his ships for flight
And plans to steal away in them by night.
    Queen Dido had a slight suspicion of this,   1290
Perceiving well that something was amiss.
So lying in his bed with sighs at night,
She asked him straight: 'Is anything not right,
My own heart's darling, whom I love the most?'
'Truly,' he said, 'tonight my father's ghost
As I was sleeping caused me torment sore,
And also Mercury* a message bore
That I am bound to conquer Italy:
To sail at once there is my destiny.
And that is why my heart is burst, it seems!'   1300
Therewith his artful tears poured down in streams
As he embraced her strongly. 'Is that true?'
She cried, 'In faith is that what you will do?
Have you not truly sworn to marry me?
What sort of woman would you make of me?
I am of rank, a queen of noble life:
You will not thus so foully leave your wife?
What shall I do? Alas that I was born!'
In brief this noble Dido, thus forlorn,
Says prayers at shrines and offers sacrifice,   1310
And piteous to tell, she kneels and cries,
She conjures him and swears that she will be

His slave, his servant of the lowest degree;
She falls before his feet and, fainting there
Dishevelled, with her bright and golden hair,
'Have mercy! Let me go with you!' she cried.
'These nobles at the court close at my side
Will kill me otherwise because of you.
But if you take me as your wife most true,
As you have sworn to, then I give you leave   1320
To kill me with your sword this very eve!
For then I shall at least die as your wife.
I am with child, so give my child his life!
Have pity in your mind, have mercy, Lord!'

   No gain at all her pleading did afford,
Because one night he left her sleeping sound
And stole away. His company he found
And sailed away from Carthage treacherously
Towards the spacious land of Italy.
So leaving Dido to her wretched life,   1330
He there acquired Lavinia as his wife.

   When he from sleeping Dido stole at night,
He left a robe, besides his sword so bright,
At her bedhead, so hasty then was he
To join his men and steal away to sea.
That robe, when hapless Dido came to wake,
She kept on kissing for its owner's sake
And said, 'Sweet robe, if Jupiter permit,
Now take my soul, let me of pain be quit!
My course of fortune I have now fulfilled.'   1340
Alas! Divine support not being willed,
She fell to fainting twenty times or more.
Her lamentations then she came to pour
Upon her sister Anne – and I shan't write
Of that, I feel such pity for her plight –
And told her sister and her nurse to go
And fetch her fire and other things, that so,
She said, she'd sacrifice: that was her aim.
Then, judging when the moment for it came,
She with his sword leaped right into the fire,   1350

And with it pierced her heart upon that pyre.
Before she stabbed herself, or death occurred,
My author says she had a final word.

    She wrote it in a letter which began:
'In just the same way as the snow-white swan
When faced with death begins to sing a song,
So I complain to you about my wrong.
Not that I think to win you back again,
For well I know that that is all in vain,
Seeing that the gods are enemies to me.   1360
But since my name is lost through you,' wrote she,
'I well may loose on you a word by letter,
Although my doing so makes me no better;
For that same wind that blew your ship away
Also blew away your faith, I say.'
You want to read that letter's every word? –
To Ovid, where it is, please be referred.

IV

The Legends of Hypsipyle and Medea, Martyrs

Duke Jason, primal source of treachery
In lovers, you who ate up guilefully
To their confusion ladies noble and pure!   1370
You captured gentlewomen with the lure
Of your high state and noble elegance,
With speeches stuffed with charm and eloquence,
And with your counterfeited constancy,
Your deference and false humility,
And with pretended pain and suffering too.
Others were false to one, but you tricked two!
O, frequently you swore that you would die
Of love, when all the harm that made you sigh
Was evil lust, and that was love, you said!   1380
My life on it, in English shall be read
Your name, and all your cunning guile be known!
Have at you, Jason! At you the horn is blown!*
Though grief and woe it bring, yet true it is

That love, when man is faithless, works like this:
False lovers have much better loving cheer
Than those who ache with love and buy it dear,
Or in the wars get many bloody knocks.
As tender capon feeds the crafty fox,
And is by him abominably betrayed,   1390
So too betrayed's the poultryman who paid,
Who to the bird had every claim and right;
But yet the false fox takes his share at night.
The truth of that in Jason's case is clear:
I cite Hypsipyle and Queen Medea.

THE LEGEND OF HYPSIPYLE

In Thessaly, so Guido* writes, there was
Long since a king whose name was Pelias
Whose brother Aeson, being at last so old
That he could hardly walk, so we are told,
Gave up to Pelias all the governing   1400
And rule, and called his brother lord and king.
This Aeson had a son called Jason who
Became the greatest knight that country knew
During his lifetime, famed for courtliness,
Largess and strength, vigour and cheerfulness.
His father being dead, so famed was he
That no one wished to be his enemy;
They praised him rather, kept his company,
Which drew from Pelias mighty jealousy.
He fearfully imagined Jason might   1410
Be elevated to such splendid height
By all the love the region's lords had shown
That he himself might well be overthrown;
So nightly all his wits he then employed
To scheme how Jason might be quite destroyed
Without himself receiving any blame.
After much thought, the right solution came:
Send Jason to some far-off country where
He'd meet his fate, and get destruction there!

197

This being decided, he made overture   1420
To Jason with much love and friendship pure
For fear that his intentions should be spied.
It so fell out, since fame spreads far and wide,
That tidings came, or that there was report,
That on an isle called Colchis,* so men thought,
Beyond Troy city, eastward in the sea,
There was a ram which, everyone could see,
Possessed a fleece of gold which shone so bright
That nowhere was there such another sight;
But yet a dragon always guarded it.   1430
And there were other marvels, I submit –
Two mighty bulls entirely made of brass
Who spat out fire: besides, much else there was.
And this is what is said concerning these:
Whoever wished to win that Golden Fleece,
Before he could possess it, first must fight
Against both bulls and dragon for that right.
Aeëtes was the monarch of the isle.

So Pelias pondered thus his course of guile:
He'd spur his nephew Jason, so he thought,   1440
To sail to Colchis to achieve that sport.
'Dear nephew, if it could arise,' said he,
'That you would win the high celebrity
Of getting that famed treasure in your hand
And bringing it back with you to my land,
It would both honour me and give me pleasure.
I should be bound to quit in fullest measure
All your pains, and all your costs I'd pay.
So choose who shall go with you on your way,
And let us see now: will you dare this quest?'   1450
Jason was young and strong and full of zest
And undertook the task without delay.
The ships, by Argus* built, got under way,
And Jason took the mighty Hercules
And other hand-picked men upon the seas.
But if you ask who else was with him gone,
Go read it in the *Argonauticon*,*

The list of men there's on a bigger scale!
So Philoctetes* hauled aloft the sail,
The wind being right for them, and fair and free   1460
It blew them from the land of Thessaly.
Long Jason sailed upon the salty sea
Until on Lemnos island landed he –
All this is not in Guido, if you please,
But Ovid wrote it in *Heroides* –
And of this island Queen Hypsipyle*
Was mistress: young and bright and fair was she,
The daughter of old Thoas, former king.
 Hypsipyle, who was a-pleasuring
And roaming on the cliffs beside the sea,   1470
Happened beneath a hillock there to see
Where Jason's ships were coming in to land.
Kind-heartedly she sent a sweet demand
To ask if any stranger blown ashore
By tempest in the night she might restore
To comfort, since it was her custom so
To succour every voyager and show
Her bounteous kindness and her courtesy.
Her messenger went straight down to the sea
And there found Jason, who with Hercules   1480
Had landed in a cock-boat at his ease,
That they might have a change and take the air,
The morning weather being mild and fair.
Advancing thus to meet those mighty lords,
The envoy greeted them with gracious words
And gave her message, asking if they'd had
Much damage or experience that was bad,
Or needed pilot or re-victualling.
If they had needs, she'd get them everything;
The Queen insisted that it should be so.   1490
 Jason replied with humble speech and low,
'I give my lady thanks most heartily
For her great kindness, but in honesty
We have no needs at present. We are tired;
To relax a bit on land's what we desired

Until the wind is right for us again.'
This lady, near the cliff with all her train
Disporting happily along the strand,
Saw Jason and this other noble stand
Explaining, as I said, why they were there.   1500
When Hercules and Jason were aware
It was the Queen, with such a lady meeting,
At once they gave her fair and gentle greeting.
She took good heed, and well did she assess
Their splendid manner, speech and style of dress,
And knew that they were men of high degree.
So to her citadel in company
Did she escort those strangers courteously,
And ask what hardships and adversity
The two had suffered on the salty sea;   1510
So that, within one day, or two, or three,
She knew from people in his ships who came
That they were Jason, man of well-known fame,
And mightier yet, most famous Hercules,
For Colchis bound, to seek the Golden Fleece,
Which made her honour both men all the more,
And dally with them longer than before.
For truly they were most distinguished folk.
Mainly it was with Hercules she spoke;
She bared her heart to him because he seemed   1520
Discreet, wise, truthful, serious, well-esteemed
And able to converse in balanced fashion
Without vile speculation or false passion.

   This Jason was by Hercules so praised
That right up to the sun's height he was raised,
So that no man was ever truer in love
Beneath the dome of heaven high above;
He was a wise man, trusty, rich and bold.
In these three things none beat him, be it told:
In vigour and free giving he surpassed   1530
All living men; the dead too he outclassed.
And third, so great and noble a man was he,
He might become the King of Thessaly.

He had no fault but that he took great fright
At love; to speak of it ashamed him quite.
He'd rather murder and be killed for it
Than be described as 'lover', he'd admit.
'If mighty God would grant it, I would give
My flesh and blood, provided I might live,
To see him certain somewhen of a wife   1540
For his estate; for what a happy life
She'd lead with this attractive, noble knight!'
    And all this thing was plotted in the night
Between this Jason and this Hercules,
Who both thought up the fraud, the crafty wheeze,
To foist themselves upon an innocent!
To fool this queen was their agreed intent.
And Jason was as bashful as a maid,
Looked pitiful, to speak was quite afraid,
But yet gave freely to her counsellors   1550
Expensive gifts, and to her officers.
Would God but grant me leisured ease and time
To detail all his wooings in my rhyme!
If in this house false lover here there be,
Then Jason there did just the same as he,
With tricks and every sort of artful deed.
You'll get no more from me, but you may read
The original, where everything is said.
    The end was this, that Jason came to wed
This queen, took what he liked without discretion   1560
Of her belongings for his own possession,
Fathered two children on her quickly, then
Set sail and never saw the queen again.
She sent a letter to him, never doubt,
Too long for me to write, or read it out,
Reproving him for lack of faith and truth,
And begging him to pity her forsooth.
She said this of her children, I declare:
That like their father were the little pair
In everything except their lack of guile.   1570
She prayed to God that in a little while,

The next time that he won a lady's heart,
She too would find he falsely did depart,
And after that would both their babies kill,
Like any others who let him have his will.
But she was true to Jason all her life,
Remaining ever taintless as his wife.
Her heart from then on knew no happiness:
She died for love of him in wretchedness.

THE LEGEND OF MEDEA

To Colchis then this noble Jason came,   1580
That dragon, that devourer of Love's flame.
As matter always yearns for form, and then
May pass from form to form, and on again,
Or as a well that's bottomless heaves ever,
False Jason quested on, and peace found never,
For longing through his lustful appetite
To have fine women was his whole delight,
The single joy he knew that pleased him well.
    Then Jason went forth to the citadel
In olden times called Jaconites and   1590
The capital of Colchis' famous land;
And there he told Aeëtes, who was King
Of Colchis, why he'd come adventuring,
And begged permission for his questing bold:
If possible, to win the Fleece of Gold.
The King agreed at once to his request,
And dealt with him as with an honoured guest,
So much so that his daughter and his heir,
Medea, a girl so sapient and fair
That no man ever saw a lovelier,   1600
He made ask Jason to sit close to her
At meals and entertainments in the hall.
    Now Jason was good-looking after all,
Was lordly too and of illustrious name,
With bearing like a lion of royal fame,
Was fluent of speech and debonair of look,

And knew concerning Love without the book,
Its art and craft, and all its duties too;
And since from Fortune harm to her was due,
She fell in love and doted on the man.   1610
'Jason,' she said, 'to judge as best I can
This enterprise which you are keen about,
You've put yourself in peril, I've no doubt.
Whoever would this mighty quest achieve
Could hardly come from it, so I believe,
Alive unless I help him with my skill.
In spite of which,' said she, 'it is my will
To advance your cause, so that you shall not die,
But go safe home again to Thessaly.'

　　'Good lady, that you might,' was Jason's word,   1620
'By death or woe of mine enjoy reward,
Yet honour me and wish my cause to serve,
Is much much more than I can well deserve
By strength or deed, while life remains my lot.
May God give thanks to you, which I cannot!
I am your man, and humbly I beseech
That you will give me help. So no more speech!
But yet, I swear, I do not flinch from death.'

　　Medea then spoke to him with urgent breath
To tell him of the dangers of his plight,   1630
One after another, in his coming fight.
She said that no one in that dreadful strife
But she herself could guarantee his life.
So briefly and directly, here's the point:
Between the two was made agreement joint
That Jason would espouse her, sworn true knight,
And at the due hour go to her at night,
And in her chamber there would swear his oath
Upon the goddess, never, like or loath,
By night or day to break his marriage faith,   1640
But stay her man while he had life and breath;
And she in turn would stop him being killed.
Thereon that night their tryst they both fulfilled.
He swore his oath and took her off to bed,

And in the morning up he gladly sped,
Because she'd taught him how he should not fail
To win the Fleece, and in the fight prevail.
She saved his life and won him honour too,
The reputation to a conqueror due,
Because she laid her strong enchantment on.   1650
   So Jason has the Fleece and home is gone,
Taking Medea and loads of treasure too
To Thessaly. Her father never knew
She'd gone off with Duke Jason whom she loved,
But who to her an evil-doer proved.
For soon he falsely left her, grief to tell,
Leaving her with their two small babes as well.
He tricked her like the traitor that he was,
The chief of Love's betrayers. Soon, alas,
To yet a third wife he was quickly tied;   1660
The daughter of King Creon was his bride.
   So that was all the love and the reward
Medea had from Jason, her false lord,
For her true faith and for her kindliness.
She loved him better than herself, I guess;
For him she left her father and her nation.
Of Jason, we may state his reputation:
In all his days there never could be found
So false a lover walking on the ground.
And therefore in her letter this wrote she,   1670
Upbraiding him for all his treachery:
'Why was I pleased to watch your yellow hair
More than the limit of my honour fair?
Why did I love you, beautiful and young
And infinitely eloquent of tongue?
O had you fallen in your battle dread,
With you much treachery would now be dead!'
In Ovid's verse her letter's set out right;
Just now, it's far too long for me to write.*

V

The Legend of Roman Lucrece, Martyr

I write now how the Kings of Rome were sent   1680
For evil-doing into banishment,
And tell of Tarquin,* last of them in date,
Whose deeds Ovid and Livy both relate.
Yet not for that cause do I tell this story,
But to memorialize and praise in glory
That perfect wife, that best in faith, Lucrece,
Whose wifely virtues and great constancies
Not only pagans sing with commendation,
But he who in our Legend's* appellation
Is known as great Augustine felt much pity   1690
For this Lucrece who died in Rome's fair city.
My tale of how it happened will be short,
For major details only I'll report.

   Now when the Romans, resolute and strong,
Had stayed besieging Ardea* so long
Without accomplishing the aim they sought,
That they became half idle, so they thought,
In joking chatter Tarquin, being young
And free and irresponsible of tongue,
Remarked that there they led a lazy life,   1700
With no man doing more fighting than his wife.
'So it is best we make our wives well known,
And each man in his fashion praise his own;
For talking thus will do our spirits good.'

   At once a knight called Collatine upstood
And spoke as follows: 'Sir, there is no need
To credit words when we can trust the deed.
I have a wife,' he said, 'and I am sure
That everyone who's met her knows she's pure.
Let's go tonight to Rome,* and we shall see.'   1710
And Tarquin answered, 'Yes, that pleases me.'
The pair arrived in Rome and made their way
To Collatine's abode without delay,
And there dismounted. Well the husband knew

The plan of his estate and ways in too,
So secretly they made an entry straight,
There being no porter watching at the gate,
And sought the noble lady's chamber door.
There by her bedside, hair unbound, they saw
Her sitting, not a thought of harm in mind,   1720
Weaving soft wool, the book says, thus inclined
To keep herself from sloth and indolence.
She urged her maids to work with diligence
And asked them, 'What's the news? What do men say
About the siege? What is expected, pray?
O, would to God the walls would tumble down!
For far too long my husband's out of town,
In dread of which my spirits burn and smart
As if a sword had pierced my very heart
When thinking of the siege or of the place.   1730
May God preserve my husband with his grace!'
And thereupon she wept in tender grieving,
Taking no more notice of her weaving,
And lowered her sad eyes submissively –
A beautifully becoming sight to see.
Her tears as well, virtuous to a degree,
Greatly adorned her wifely chastity;
Her expression and her heart were in one mode,
In harmony with what they did and showed.
And as she spoke, before she was aware,   1740
Her husband Collatine came straight in there
And said, 'Don't be afraid, for I am here!'
And she arose at once with joyful cheer
And kissed him, as good wives are wont to do.

  The King's son, Tarquin, arrogant through and through,
Struck by her beauty and her lovely face,
Her golden hair, her mien, her body's grace,
Her sweet look, and the way that she lamented,
(Her loveliness was not by art augmented)*
Conceived for her as violent a desire   1750
As if his heart were suddenly on fire.
So mad he was, his reason was undone,

Yet well he knew that she would not be won;
Which plunged him all the deeper in despair
The more he wanted her and thought her fair.
He lusted for her with blind coveting.
    Next morning, when the birds began to sing,
He stole back to the siege in secrecy
And paced about alone abstractedly,
Her image ever fresh within his mind.   1760
'Thus was her look, and thus her hair was twined;
Thus sat she, talked and spun, thus looked her face,
Thus lovely was she, such her moving grace.'
With these ideas his heart was freshly taken.
And as the sea, by tempest tossed and shaken,
After the stormy gale has ceased to blow
Still heaves with waves another day or two,
Just so, although her body was not there,
Its pleasing qualities most truly were.
It did not only please, but roused in spite   1770
Malicious lust, immoral in delight.
'Will she, nill she, I'll get her into bed:
Luck helps the bold man every time,' he said.
'Whatever happens, that is what I'll do.'
He girded on his sword and off he flew,
Riding to Rome without the least delay.
Then all alone he went his secret way
Directly to the house of Collatine.
The light had gone, the sun had ceased to shine;
And stealing furtively from nook to nook   1780
Tarquin through the night stalked like a crook,
When everybody had retired to bed,
And thought of treason entered no one's head.
By window or some other entry place,
With sword in hand, this Tarquin came apace
To where Lucrece the true wife lay at rest.
And as she woke, she felt her bed being pressed.
'What beast,' she cried, 'weighs down so hard on me?'
'I am the King's son, Tarquin,' answered he,
'And if you cry, or any sound let fall,   1790

Or if there wakes up anyone at all,
I swear by God, who made us one and all,
I'll thrust this sword right through your heart, I shall.'
Which said, he seized her by the throat and pressed
The sharp point of his sword against her breast.
She had no strength to speak; her tongue was dumb;
What could she say, her mind and sense being numb?
Just like a lamb found by a wolf alone,
To whom could she appeal or make her moan?
What! Should she battle with a sturdy knight?   1800
Men know a woman has no strength to fight.
What! Should she scream? How could she wrench apart
His throttle-grip, his sword being at her heart?
She begs for mercy, pleading all she can.
'You won't get that,' replies the cruel man.
'As sure as Jupiter my soul shall save,
I shall go out and kill your stable-knave,
And put him in your bed, and loudly cry
I found you in that foul adultery.
And so you will be dead, and also lose   1810
Your honour. You have nothing else to choose.'

 Now Roman wives so cherished their fair name
In olden days, so shrank at thought of shame,
That what with dread of slander and fear of death,
She lost at once her senses and her breath
And fell into a swoon so deep and dead
You could have chopped her arm off, or her head,
And she feel nothing, neither foul nor fair.

 Now Tarquin, you a king's son, royal heir,
Who should by lineage and sense of right   1820
Act as a lord and as a faithful knight,
Why have you scorned the code of chivalry?
Why have you done this lady villainy?
Alas! In you this was a shameful deed!

 But to the purpose. In the book I read,
When he had done his wickedness and gone,
This lady called together everyone,
Friends, father, mother, husband, one and all,

And pitiful to behold sat in the hall,
Her lovely bright hair all dishevelled, attired   1830
As women's mourning custom then required
When friends were taken to the burial-ground.
They asked her what had caused her woe profound,
And why she sat in tears, and who was dead.
In utter shame, no single word she said,
Nor dared she raise her eyes to them. At last
She spoke of Tarquin and of what had passed,
The event so pitiful and horrible.
To tell that grief would be impossible,
That pain in which her friends and she were thrown. 1840
Had all those people's hearts been made of stone
They would have pitied her with tenderness,
Her heart being full of truth and wifeliness.
She said that through her guilt and through her blame
Her husband should not gain an evil name;
She would not let that happen, come what may.
And they all swore in truest faith that they
Forgave her, which they knew the proper course,
Since she was guiltless, being compelled by force;
And many an example then they named,   1850
But all to no avail, for she exclaimed,
'Forgiveness may be given as you say,
But I shall not accept it any way.'
And secretly she then drew out a knife
And, stabbing with it, robbed herself of life.
And as she fell she cast a heedful eye
On how her skirts fell and were seen to lie:
Yes, in her falling she took special care
Her feet or other parts should not show bare,
Her love of shamefast honour was so great.   1860
The whole of Rome felt pity for her fate,
And Brutus* took an oath by her chaste blood
That Tarquin should be banished thence for good
With all his kin; then called the populace
And openly informed them of the case,
And openly exposed her on her bier

All round the town, that men might see and hear
The horrid facts of her dishonouring.
Nor has there ever been in Rome a king
Since then: they made of her a saint whose day*   187C
Was kept each year in a most hallowed way
By custom. Thus the records of Lucrece,
That noble wife, as Livy tells them, cease.

   I tell her tale because she was so true
That in her love she would not change for new,
And she'd a constant heart, demure and kind,
That in such women men can always find.
Where once they set their heart, it always stays.
For I assure you, Christ himself well says.
That wide as is the Land of Israel,   1880
He never found great faith maintained so well
As in a woman:* this is not a lie.
And as for men, observe what tyranny
They always practise; test them as we must,
The truest of them is too weak to trust.

VI

The Legend of Ariadne of Athens

Now judge infernal, Cretan king,*
It is your turn, so come into the ring!
I do not tell the tale for your sole sake,
But more to keep the memory awake
Of Theseus's immense bad faith in love,   1890
For which the gods who rule in heaven above
Were furious and wreaked vengeance for your sin.
Beware, for shame! Your tale I now begin.

   Minos, who was the mighty King of Crete,
And ruled a hundred cities strong and great,
To Athens sent to school Androgeus,*
His son, to whom – alas! – it happened thus:
That he was killed learning philosophy
For no more reason at all than jealousy.
So mighty Minos, he of whom I speak,   1900

Dire vengeance for his son's death came to wreak.
Megara* he besieged both hard and long,
But yet the walls were so extremely strong
And Nisus, King there, was so bold and brave,
That little cause for fear the onset gave.
Nisus felt scorn for Minos and his forces
Until one day it chanced by Fortune's courses
That Nisus' daughter,* standing on the wall,
Observed the siege in progress, saw it all.
It happened during skirmishing that she   1910
Fell deep in love with Minos suddenly,
And was so smitten with his chivalry
And beauty that she thought that she must die.
To cut the story short, she made him win
The siege by letting all his forces in,
So that he had the city at his will,
And all the people there, to save or kill.
But foul reward he gave her kindliness,
Letting her drown in sorrow and distress
Until the god took pity on her state –   1920
A tale too long for me now to relate.
Besides Alcathoë, King Minos won
Athens and other cities many a one.
The effect was, Minos rigorously
Oppressed the Athenians, who annually
Were forced to yield to him their offspring dear
For sacrifice, as you shall shortly hear.
This Minos had a monstrous wicked beast*
So cruel that he'd make an instant feast
Of any human being brought to him;   1930
There was no good defence, he was so grim.
When every third year came, as sure as sure,
By casting lots it fell to rich and poor
To take their sons, as chance might then dictate,
And give them to King Minos, when their fate
Would be to be preserved alive or killed,
Or eaten by the monster, as he willed.
And this did Minos do in deadly spite;

To avenge his son was his entire delight,
And to enslave the Athenians in this way   1940
From year to year until his dying day.
Thus home he sailed, the city being won.
This wicked custom went on being run
Until Aegeus,* the Athenian king,
Was forced to give his son as offering,
Young Theseus, when the lottery was run,
To be devoured, for mercy was there none.
And so this sad young knight was sent away
Into King Minos' court without delay,
And chained and in a dungeon thrown until   1950
He should be eaten at the monster's will.

    Well may you weep, O wretched Theseus,
And you a king's son, to be fated thus!
It seems to me you would be much in debt
To one who saved you from that deadly threat!
And if a woman were to help you now,
You ought to serve her with a faithful vow
And year by year to love her constantly!
But let me now resume my history.
The gloomy cell where Theseus had been thrown   1960
Was at the bottom of a tower deep down,
Adjacent to a privy in the wall
Which both of Minos' daughters used, for all
Their dwelling quarters with their chambers great
Were over them and faced the major street;
And there they lived in happiness and grace.
I don't know how, but still it was the case,
As Theseus at night was sorrowing,
That Ariadne, daughter of the King,
And her sister Phaedra listened to all   1970
His grieving as they stood upon the wall,
Gazing upwards at the brilliant moon
Because they hated going to bed too soon;
And they took pity on his heavy woe.
A king's son to be shut in prison so
And be devoured! It seemed to them a shame.

Then Ariadne spoke her sister's name;
'Phaedra,' she whispered, 'darling sister dear,
This royal scion's grieving – can't you hear
How sadly he laments his lofty race,   1980
Being so cast down in such a wretched place,
And guiltless? It is pitiful to me!
And so, upon my oath, if you agree,
He shall be saved, whatever else we do.'
Phaedra replied, 'Yes, truly I grieve too,
As much as ever I did for any man;
And my advice, to help as best I can,
Is that we make his guard immediately
Come up and speak with us most secretly,
And bring with him that miserable knight.   1990
For if he beats the monster in a fight,
The prize must be that he can then go free.
So let us test his spirit's bravery
And find out whether he would boldly dare
To save his life if given a sword to bear
For self-defence, and with the beast contend.
For in that dungeon where he must descend,
You know the monster's lair is in a place
That is not dark, and has sufficient space
To wield an axe or sword or staff or knife,   2000
So that I think he well may save his life.
If he's a proper man, he should do so.
And we shall also make him balls of tow
And wax, so when the monster's maw gapes wide,
Theseus can aim and throw them deep inside,
To slake his hunger and gum up his teeth.
And when he chokes and cannot get his breath,
Theseus shall leap on him with mighty blows
And strike him dead before they grapple close.
The warder shall beforehand without fail   2010
In secret hide the weapon in the gaol.
And since the labyrinth has twists and bends
And artful passageways and strange dead ends,
Just like a maze, most craftily designed –

This is the right solution to my mind –
Then he must trail a clew of twine behind
When going in, and coming out thus find
The way he came by following the thread.
And when he's struck the dreadful monster dead,
He then can flee and leave the fearful place,   2020
And take the gaoler too, whom he can raise
To some position in his land at home,
Since of such a noble line he's come.
If he dare do it, that's what I advise.'
    Why spin it out, or longer sermonize?
The gaoler comes, and Theseus with him too,
And all agree the things they have to do.
Then down goes knightly Theseus on his knee:
'Most noble lady of my life,' says he,
'I, wretched castaway condemned to death,   2030
Declare that while I shall have life or breath,
After this exploit I'll not go away,
But faithful in your service ever stay,
And as a low-born person undistinguished
Be true to you until my life's extinguished.
I shall forsake my native heritage
And in your court be, as I said, a page,
If you will let it fall within your grace
So far as to allow it in this place
That I may have my food and drink, no more.   2040
And for that sustenance I'll work therefore
As you instruct me, so that nobody –
Not Minos, who has not set eyes on me,
Nor any other – shall be aware of me,
I shall conduct myself so carefully.
I'll smirch myself and be so humbly low
That who I am no one alive could know,
To take my life; and thus I'll strive to be
With you, who did me such a charity.
This most deserving man, your gaoler now,   2050
I'll send home to my father, who, I vow,
Shall so reward him that he soon shall be

In Greece among the men of high degree.
For if I may assert it, lady bright,
I am a king's son and, besides, a knight,
And if it were God's pleasure that all three
Of you might in my native country be,
And I with you to keep you company,
Whether I'm lying you would quickly see.
If I don't serve you humbly in this place,   2060
I pray to Mars to do me such a grace
That shameful death may fall on me, and death
And want afflict my friends in that same breath,
And that my spirit after death may go
And wander nightly, walking to and fro,
And may I ever bear a traitor's name,
For which my ghost shall walk, to do me shame!
And if I ever claim a higher estate   2070
Without your offering a thing so great,
As I have said, then may I die in shame!
Your mercy, Lady! Nothing else I claim.'
    A gracious knight was Theseus to behold,
And young, being only twenty-three years old.
Yes, anyone who'd seen his face would weep
In pity for the oath he'd sworn to keep;
So that's why Ariadne gave him cheer
About his pledge, in answer kind and clear:
'A king's son and a noble knight,' said she,   2080
'To be my slave in such a low degree!
May God forbid it, for all women's shame,
And stop me ever making such a claim!
But may he send you grace of heart and skill
In self-defence, and power your foe to kill,
And grant it to me afterwards to find
That I grieve not for having saved your life!
Yet it were better I should be your wife,
Since you are quite as nobly born as I,   2090
And have a realm conveniently close by,
Than that I should allow you, innocent,
To die or be a slave in languishment.

There's no dynastic gain in that, it's clear,
But what's the thing man will not do in fear?
And as my sister, if I leave this place,
Must also go, as truly is the case,
Since she as well as I would suffer death
If both of us stayed here, now plight your faith
To wed her to your son when home you go.   2100
This matter can be well concluded so;
Promise it now, by all that may be sworn.'
'I swear, my lady. If I fail, then torn,'
He said, 'by the Minotaur tomorrow may I be!
Take from my heart some blood for surety
If you desire; had I some knife or spear,
I'd let it out, and thereon I could swear,
For then I know you'd credit what I say.
By Mars, the chief of gods to whom I pray,
If I might live and haply not succumb   2110
When tomorrow's battle time shall come,
I never would depart from here before
You've seen fulfilled the solemn oath I swore.
For now, if it's the truth that I should say,
I've been in love with you for many a day
Back home in Greece, and longed to see you near,
(Although of that you'd simply no idea)
Preferring you to all things else alive.
I swear upon my faith, as I may thrive,
For seven years I've served you faithfully.   2120
Now I have you, and also you have me,
My dearest heart, Duchess of Athens now!'
    The lady smiled at his most heartfelt vow
And at his constancy and noble cheer,
And to her sister said as you shall hear
With gentle speech: 'Now sister mine,' said she,
'Both you and I are duchesses, and we
In Athens' royal line shall be secure,
And soon be queens thereafter, I am sure.
We've saved from death a prince of kingly name –   2130
And noble women by custom always aim

To save a noble man if they've the force,
And he has right, and runs an honest course.
For this I think no man should give us blame
Or fix upon us any evil name.'
　　To make the matter I am telling brief,
This Theseus of the ladies took his leave,
And every detail was performed in deed
As in their compact you have heard me read.
His sword, his clew, his things, as I have said,　　　2140
Were in the building by the gaoler laid,
Close to the lair where lived the Minotaur,
Where Theseus would go in, beside the door.
So to his death this Theseus was sent,
And forth in to the Minotaur he went,
And worked the plan that Ariadne taught,
And beat and killed the monster when they fought,
And following the clew came out again
In secret when the Minotaur was slain,
And through the gaoler procured a barge,　　　2150
And loaded Ariadne's treasure large,
And took wife, sister, gaoler, all three,
On board, and softly stole away to sea,
Sailing under cover of the night,
And safely in Aegina* did alight,
Where Theseus had a good friend, as it chanced.
And there they feasted, there they sang and danced,
And he had Ariadne in his arms
Who'd saved him from the monster and death's harms.
He soon acquired another ship again　　　2160
And with a host of fellow-countrymen
He took his leave; and homeward then sailed he.
But on an isle* amid the fierce sea,
Where living man or being dwelled there none
But savage creatures many and many a one,
He put his ship ashore for a brief stay,
And paused and idled there for half a day,
Saying he had to have a rest on land.
His mariners complied with his command

And -- briefly then my story to expound --   2170
While Ariadne lay in sleep profound,
Thinking her sister lovelier than she,
He took her by the hand and treacherously
Led her on board the ship, and stole away,
Leaving Ariadne where she lay,
And happily towards Athens set his sails --
May he be blown by twenty devils' gales! --
And found his father had been drowned at sea.
By God! You'll hear no more of him from me!
   These faithless lovers, poison be their bane!   2180
To Ariadne let me turn again,
Still fast asleep, worn out with weariness.
Her heart will wake in misery, I guess.
Alas! For you in pity beats my heart!
She woke up in the dawn light with a start
And groping round, found nothing in the bed.
'Alas that ever I was born!' she said,
'I am betrayed!' And then she tore her hair
And ran down to the beach, her feet all bare,
Exclaiming, 'Theseus, my sweetheart true,   2190
Where are you, that I cannot be with you?
Alone among wild beasts I'm left to die.'
The hollow rocks with echoes made reply.
She saw no man, and still there shone the moon.
Then high upon a rock she climbed up soon
And saw his vessel sailing out at sea.
Her heart went cold, and thus aloud said she:
'Kinder than you are creatures of the wild!'
Did he not sin, to leave her so beguiled?
She cried out, 'O turn back, for pity and sin.   2200
Your vessel has not all its company in!'
She tied her head-scarf to a pole up high,
In hope perhaps that it would catch his eye,
And tell him she had been abandoned and
Make him return and find her on the strand.
But all for nothing; on his way he'd gone,
And she fell down and swooned upon a stone.

Then up she rose and kissed with loving care
His footprints where they lay before her there,
And spoke these words directly to their bed: 2210
'Thou bed which hast received a pair,' she said,
'Thou shalt reply for two, and not for one!
Alas! Where has the greater partner gone?
What shall become – alas! – of wretched me?
For though a ship may put in from the sea,
I dare not go back home for very dread.
No good expedient comes into my head.'
Shall I tell on her further lamentation?
It would produce a tedious narration.
In her *Epistle* Ovid gives it all,   2220
But tell it briefly to the end I shall.
The gods delivered her in sympathy,
And in the sign of Taurus* men may see
The jewels of her coronet shining bright.
And here's the last of this that I shall write:
May the devil soon requite a fickle lover
Who cheats a true betrothed and throws her over!

VII

The Legend of Philomela

Creator of all forms, who well designed
And made fair earth, and had it in your mind
Eternally, before your work began!   2230
How could you so create, in shame of man,
Or, if it was not your engendering,
Permit such consequence? To do a thing
Like letting that foul Tereus be born,
Who was so false in love and so forsworn,
The uttering of whose name invites decay
From Earth below to Primum Mobile!*
And as for me, so ghastly was his deed
That every time his grisly tale I read
My eyes go dim and suffer ugly pains.   2240
The poison of so long ago remains,

Infecting everyone who would behold
The words of Tereus' tale, of which I told.
    He was the Lord of Thrace, and Mars's kin,
That cruel god with bloody javelin;
And he had married in abundant cheer
The King Pandion's* lovely daughter dear
Called Procne, fairest flower in all of Thrace.
Their wedding, Juno* was not pleased to grace,
Nor Hymen,* god of marriage, but instead,   2250
With all their killing torches burning red,
The Furies Three* were at the celebration.
All night upon the beams the Owl* kept station,
The prophet of despair and of mischance.
The revels, full of happy song and dance,
Went on a fortnight, or a little less,
But all the details I must now compress
Because I am so weary of the man.
Five years his marriage with this Procne ran
Until one day she longed, it so appears,   2260
To see the sister she'd not seen for years;
She longed so much, she knew not what to say.
Then to her husband did she keenly pray,
For love of God, that she might go and see
Her sister and return immediately,
Or let her sister come and visit her,
And he send word to her by messenger.
Day after day her humble prayer she pressed
With wifely speech and humour of the best.
    This Tereus equipped his ships for sea,   2270
And into Grecian waters forth sailed he,
And not long after of his father-in-law
He begged that he would let, for a month or more,
His sister-in-law, Philomela,* come
To Procne his wife and visit her at home –
'And she will soon rejoin you, I aver.
Myself I'll take her and return with her,
And guard her like my life's heart-blood, no less.'
    Pandion, this old king, in tenderness

Of heart began at once to weep and grieve 2280
That he should give his Philomela leave:
Nothing in all this world did he love so.
But finally she got his leave to go,
For Philomela, salt tears on her face,
In trying hard to win her father's grace
To see again the sister she adored,
Embraced him. Such a sight did she afford
When doing that, so lovely did she seem
To Tereus, so youthfully a-gleam,
While in her dress she was the nonpareil, 2290
And yet in beauty twice as rich as well,
He fixed his fiery heart on her and meant
To have her soon, however matters went.
And so in craft he kneeled as well, and prayed
Till at the last Pandion sighed and said,
'Now son-in-law, who are to me so dear,
I trust to you my younger daughter here,
Who bears the key to all my heart and life.
Commend me to my daughter and your wife,
And may she spend her time in pleasure high: 2300
But let her see me once before I die.'
And truly then he made a sumptuous feast
For Tereus and his men, the best and least
Attending him; and gave him presents fair,
And led him down the chiefest thoroughfare
Of Athens, and then brought him to the sea,
And turned back home. He thought no villainy.

   The oarsmen drew the vessel forward fast,
And safe in Thrace they all arrived at last,
And up into a forest then they sped, 2310
And her into a secret cave he led,
And in that cavern dark he made request
That, would she or not, she there must take a rest.
She shuddered in her heart and then spoke thus:
'Where is my sister, brother Tereus?'
And thereupon she wept most feelingly
And, pale with fear, she quaked most piteously

Exactly like the lamb the wolf has bitten,
Or like the dove the eagle once has smitten,
Who somehow wriggles from the claws' grim hold, 2320
Yet lies confounded and in terror cold
Lest she be seized again; yes, so sat she.
But it was clear no other fate could be.
By force the traitor did the shameful deed
And took away from her her maidenhead
Against her will with violent assault.
Lo! Here's a man's deed, typical man's fault.
'Sister!' she screamed, and cried in accents clear,
'Help me, God in heaven!' and 'Father dear!'
To no avail; and then this thieving traitor   2330
Did her damage infinitely greater
For fear lest she should cry abroad his shame
And do him harm by slandering his name.
He cut her tongue out with his sword and then
He shut her in a castle far from men,
And locked her in a secret prison there
For use and pleasure when he wished, I swear,
To keep her from escaping evermore.
O luckless Philomel, with heart so sore!
May God avenge you and fulfil your prayer!   2340
And now it's time I ended this affair.
    Tereus then returned to his own place
And, giving to his wife a close embrace,
He wept most piteously and shook his head,
And swore that he had found her sister dead;
Which gave this hapless Procne such deep woe,
Her heart with grieving almost broke in two.
Now, Procne thus I leave in tearful gloom
So that her sister's tale I may resume.
This noble lady had been taught, in truth,   2350
To sew and to embroider in her youth,
And to weave tapestry upon a frame,
As once was woman's custom and her fame.
Of food and drink she was allowed her fill,
And had whatever clothes might please her will.

Now she could read, compose and also spell,
But writing with a pen she did not well.*
Yet she could weave the letters to and fro,
So by the time a year had passed in woe
She'd woven in coarse wool a pictured note   2360
How she'd been brought from Athens in a boat,
How she'd been taken to the cave alone,
And everything that Tereus had done.
She wove it well, and wrote the story above
How she'd been served for showing her sister love.
And to a servant then she gave a ring,
And begged him* with her signs to go and bring
To Procne what she'd woven on the cloth.
By signs she swore to him with many an oath
That she'd reward him then as best she could.   2370
Off to the Queen then sped this servant good,
And showed it her, and all its story told.
When Procne came the tapestry to behold,
She said no word in sorrow or in rage,
But feigned at once to go on pilgrimage
To Bacchus' temple; and not far from there
Found her dumb sister sitting in despair
And weeping in the castle, all alone.
Alas! the pitiful lament, the moan
That Procne made of Philomela's harms!   2380
Each sister took the other in her arms,
And thus I leave them in their sorrow dwelling.
    As for the rest, no burden is the telling.
That's all there is.* For that's how she was served,
Who from this cruel man no harm deserved,
Nor did him wrong of which she was aware.
So, if you please, of man you should beware,
For though he would not wish, for very shame,
To do as Tereus did, and lose his name,
Nor serve you as a murderer or knave,   2390
He won't for long in faithful style behave –
I'll say it now, although he were my brother –
Unless as lover he can't get another!

VIII

The Legend of Phyllis

By proof as well as by authority,
A wicked fruit comes from a wicked tree:
That's what you find, by my analysis.
The reason I now mention it is this:
To tell the tale of faithless Demophon.*
So fickle in love I heard of only one,
And that one was his father Theseus.   2400
'From such, may God in mercy succour us!'
Yes, that's how women ought to pray who know.
Now straight into my story I must go.

    With Troy destroyed and ruined utterly,
Demophon came sailing on the sea
Towards Athens, to his palace high and large,
And with him many a ship and many a barge
Full of his troops, of whom too many a one
Were badly wounded, sick or woebegone,
As at the Siege of Troy they long had lain.   2410
Behind him came a gale and storm of rain
Much fiercer than his rigging could withstand:
He'd give the universe to be on land,
The storm so chased him to and fro with force!
So dark it was, he could not set a course.
The rudder, smashed by waves, all useless hung,
And leaks below the water-line were sprung;
No carpenter could put such damage right.
Like burning torch the sea boiled up at night
Like mad, and heaved the ship now up, now down, 2420
Till Neptune* out of pity ceased to frown,
With Thetis,* Chorus and with Triton,* all
Of whom then caused him on a coast to fall,
Where Phyllis was the mistress and the queen,
Lycurgus'* daughter, of more lovely mien
Than is the flower beside the brilliant sun.
Scarce had Demophon his landing won,
Exhausted, weak and feeble, with his crew

Worn out with weariness and famished too,
Than all became aware that he might die. 2430
His sage advisers told him he should try
To seek some help and succour from the Queen,
Discovering thus what favour he might win,
What profit he could manage in that land
All chance of woe and hardship to withstand.
For he was ill and at the point of death,
And he could hardly speak or draw his breath.
And so he stayed in Rhodope* to rest.
When he could walk, it seemed by far the best
To go to court and there seek royal aid, 2440
For he was known; to him respect was paid
Because of Athens Duke and Lord was he
Like Theseus, his father, previously,
Who in his time commanded mighty fame,
And in that region had the greatest name.
And he was like his sire in face and stature,
And also false in love: it came by nature,
Like Reynard the Fox's father's handing on
Of his own craft and nature to his son
Without instruction, as a duck can swim 2450
When carried new-born to the water's brim.
    This honourable Phyllis liked his face
And manner, and warmly greeted him with grace.
But since I'm altogether surfeited
With writing out what faithless lovers did,
I'll tell the legend at a spanking pace,
Which to perform, God send me ample grace!
And this is how I'll tell it in a tick:
You've heard the tale of Theseus' nasty trick
In falsely leaving Ariadne fair, 2460
Whose pity saved him in the monster's lair?
Well, briefly, just the same was Demophon,
Going the same way, falsely treading on
The same path that his father Theseus trod.
To Phyllis thus he swore by every god
To marry her, and pledged fidelity.

225

He did his best to filch her property
When he was well and by his resting eased,
And did with Phyllis wholly what he pleased;
And if I pleased, then I could well proceed   2470
To chart his to's and fro's and every deed.

   He had to sail back home, is what he said,
To furnish all the things required to wed
Her as her state required, and his as well.
That done, straightforwardly he bade farewell,
Swearing he'd not delay in this concern,
But would for sure within a month return.
In Rhodope he took the dues of rank
And like a lord received obeisance frank
As if he were at home, fitted his fleet,   2480
And to his own land beat a fast retreat.
To Phyllis, however, he never came again,
And that she bore with agony and pain.
Alas! As all the old accounts record,
She killed herself by strangling with a cord
When she perceived that Demophon was false.
But first she wrote, and sent him urgent calls
To come to her and rid her of her woe,
Of which I shall report a word or two.
I shall not sweat for him, or so I think,   2490
Nor pen on him one dip-full of my ink,
For he was false in love as was his sire.
And may the Devil set both their souls on fire!
But of poor Phyllis's letter I shall write
A word or two, though short the account and slight:
'I am hostess to you, O Demophon,
Your Phyllis, who is now so woebegone,
Of Rhodope, and must to you complain
About the terms agreed between us twain,
To which in spite of oaths you don't adhere.   2500
You dropped your anchor in our harbour here,
And promised us that you'd return as soon
As, or before, there'd passed a monthly moon.
But four times more the moon has hid her face

226

Since that day you departed from this place,
And also four times lit the world with light.
And yet, if I observe the truth aright,
The ocean stream of Thrace has still not brought
Your ship from Athens; come here it does not.
And if you count that period as you should,   2510
As I or any faithful lover would,
You'll see I don't complain before it's due.'
But I don't give her whole epistle to you
In order, which would make hard work for me,
For it was long, and penned expansively.
But here and there I've versified her plea
When what she wrote seemed quite well said to me.
She wrote to him, 'Your sails don't come again:
To look for faith in what you said is vain.
And I know why you do not come,' wrote she.   2520
'With loving favours I was much too free.
As for the gods by whom you falsely swore,
If their vengeance falls on you therefore,
You won't be strong enough to bear the pain.
I placed too much reliance, I complain,
On your high rank and on your pleasing tongue,
And on your tears, from eyes so slyly wrung.
How could you weep so falsely?' she complained.
'And could such tears as those be really feigned?
Now truly, if you think the matter through,   2530
It ought to bring but little fame to you
To have deceived like this a simple maid!
I pray to God, and I have often prayed,
That this may be your greatest glory due,
And highest honour that shall fall to you.
And when your ancient ancestors are painted,
And men are with their noble deeds acquainted,
I pray to God that you are painted too,
And people may observe there as they view,
"Look, here's the man who with his flattery   2540
Betrayed a maid and did her villainy,
Although her love was true in thought and deed!"

227

But truly, of one fact they're bound to read:
That you are like your father in your shame,
For he tricked Ariadne just the same,
With just such craft and just such subtlety
As you yourself have just deluded me.
And in that matter, which is far from fair,
You truly follow him and are his heir.
But since you've hoodwinked me so sinfully,   2550
My body you are shortly going to see
Float into Athens harbour on the wave,
Without a proper burial or grave,
Although you are much harder than a stone.'
The letter was sent off and, left alone,
She felt how fickle and how false he was,
And in despair she hanged herself, alas!
Such store she set on him, and felt such woe.
Beware, you women, of your subtle foe,
Since still today such bad men you may see;   2560
And trust in love no other man but me.

IX

The Legend of Hypermnestra

In Greece there were two brothers long ago,
And one was called Danaus, you should know,
Who with his body sired a host of sons —
False lovers often are such clever ones! —
Among which progeny there was a son
He loved much more than any other one.
And when this son was born, Danaus thus
Proposing, named the infant Lynceus.
Aegyptus was the other brother's name;*   2570
Promiscuous he, as if it were a game.
And he sired many daughters in his life,
But one, whom he begat upon his wife,
A cherished daughter whom he chose to call
Hypermnestra, youngest of them all,
By chance of stars at her nativity

Gained every good and lovely quality,
As if the gods had ruled when she was born
That of the sheaf this girl should be the corn.
The Fates, those beings we call Destiny,   2580
So crafted her that she was bound to be
Kind and serious, true as steel and wise –
All of them good women's qualities.
Though Venus gave great loveliness to her,
She was compounded under Jupiter
And so had conscience, loyalty, dread of shame,
And the desire to guard her virtue's fame.
All these she thought meant happiness for her.
Red Mars was at that special time of year
So feeble that his malice had declined;   2590
The rise of Venus cramped his cruel mind
So that, with her and many another star
Pressuring him, his bile was less by far.
So Hypermnestra could not wield a knife
In anger, no, though she should lose her life.
But from the turning heavens, all the same
To her from Saturn two bad aspects came,
Which caused her afterwards to die in gaol,
Concerning which I'll later tell the tale.

　　Danaus and Aegyptus then agreed –   2600
Though they were brothers of the selfsame seed,
For then it was not wrong to marry thus –
To bring together in marriage Lynceus
And Hypermnestra, their two offspring dear,
And chose the day to which they would adhere,
And all was settled, as I understand.
The time was near, the arrangements well in hand.
This Lynceus took in marriage his father's brother's
Daughter, and they so became each other's.
The torches flamed, the lamps were burning bright, 2610
The sacrifices all prepared aright;
Sweet from the fire the incense smell did shoot;
The flower and leaf were torn up by the root
To make the garlands and the lofty crowns.

And minstrelsy filled all the place with sounds
Of amorous songs devised for wedding days
According to that period's simple ways.
Aegyptus' palace was the place for this,
Where he did what he liked, for it was his.
And so they revelled till day's end was come,   2620
And then the guests took leave and trooped off home;
And night being come, the bride was bound for bed.
Aegyptus to his chamber quickly sped,
And secretly he bade his daughter call.
The palace being emptied of them all,
He gazed upon his daughter with good cheer,
And said to her as you shall quickly hear:
'Dear daughter mine, and treasure of my heart,
Since first I had a shirt at my life's start,
That day the Fatal Sisters* shaped my doom,   2630
So near my heart has nothing ever come
As you, my Hypermnestra, daughter dear.
Ponder what I, your father, tell you here,
And what my greater wisdom bids you, do,
For, daughter, first of all, I love you so
That all the world's not half so dear to me.
I'd not advise you to your misery
For all the gain beneath the cold bright moon.
What I intend I'll tell you now, not soon,
With urgent affirmation, in this way: 2640
Unless you do exactly as I say
You shall be dead, by him who made us all!
You shan't escape outside my palace wall
Alive, to put it briefly, understand,
Unless you agree to do what I command!
And that is final: you must take it so.'

   This Hypermnestra cast her eyes down low
And shuddered like a leaf of aspen green,
Her colour dead, and ashen-grey her mien,
Saying, 'Lord and father, all your will,   2650
If I can, God knows, I shall fulfil,
Provided I am brought to no disgrace.'

He rapped back, 'No proviso in this case!'
And swiftly drew a dagger razor-keen.
'Hide this, and be quite sure it isn't seen;
And when your husband is in bed with you,
While he is sleeping, cut his throat in two.
For in my dreams a warning came to me
Which said my nephew would my killer be;
Which one I know not, so I'll be secure.   2660
If you refuse, we two shall quarrel, for sure,
As I have said, and sworn by God before.

    Poor Hypermnestra, out of mind therefore,
Got his permission to depart the place
And not be harmed. That was his only grace.
Producing next a little phial, he
Then said, 'A draught of this, or two or three,
Given him when he wishes to retire,
Will make him sleep as long as you desire,
The opium and narcotics are so strong.   2670
Now go, in case he thinks you stay too long.'
Out came the bride, and with a serious face,
Which virgins wear at such a time and place,
To her chamber went with revel and with song.
And briefly, lest my tale be thought too long,
This Lynceus and she were brought to bed,
And all the revellers from the chamber sped.

    The night wore on and soon he fell asleep.
Most tenderly she then began to weep;
She rose up from her bed, with horror quaking,   2680
Just like a branch the strong west wind is shaking,
While all of Argos was in silence lost.
And now she grew as cold as any frost;
For in her heart pity was labouring so,
And dread of death was causing her such woe,
She fell down thrice in misery and despair,
Yet rose again and staggered here and there,
And stared at her two hands with fixity.
'Alas! Shall these be bloodstained?' sorrowed she,
'A virgin and by nature disinclined   2690

231

Both by my wedding robes and state of mind,
And by my hands, not meant to bear a knife,
I cannot, will not, rob a man of life.
What the devil have I with this knife to do?
Or shall I let my throat be cut in two?
Then I shall bleed, alas! and die in shame!
But this thing must be settled all the same,
And either he or I must lose our life.
And out of doubt,' she said, 'since I'm his wife
And faithful, it is better far for me   2700
To die in honour and wifely chastity
Than live a traitor in undying shame.
Be as it may, in earnest or in game,
He shall awake, arise and flee away
Through this gutter, before the break of day.'
She wept most tenderly upon his face
And in her arms she held him in embrace,
And shook and woke him with a motion soft.
He leaped down from a window up aloft
When warned by her and succoured from disaster. 2710
This Lynceus was light-footed, no man faster,
And from his wife he ran at furious speed.
The luckless woman was so weak indeed,
And helpless too, that she had not gone far
Before her cruel father seized her. Ah!
Lynceus, alas! Why are you so unkind?
Why didn't you especially keep in mind
The need to take her with you safe and sound?
For when she saw that he had gone, and found
She could not catch him up, nor go his pace, 2720
Nor follow him, she sat down in that place
Until they caught and threw her chained in gaol,
And here is the conclusion of the tale.*

NOTES

THE BOOK OF THE DUCHESS

LINE

37 Eight years is a conventional period, though a few commentators see in it an autobiographical reference.

63 The story of Ceyx and Alcyone is in Book XI of Ovid's *Metamorphoses*. There, the pair are turned into sea birds through the gods' compassion and live and mate happily. The halcyon is the fabled bird during whose nesting time on the water the weather stays calm.

109 Juno (*Gr.* Hera): Queen of Heaven, consort of Jupiter (Zeus).

136 Morpheus: god of sleep and *shaper* of dreams, hence his name.

167 Enclimpostair: son of the god of sleep? There is uncertainty about the name, for which Greek and even early French etymological sources have been suggested.

255 Rennes: the town in Brittany then famed for its linen.

281 For Joseph and his interpretation of Pharaoh's dream, see Genesis 41.

284 Macrobius (*c.* 400 AD): edited Cicero's *Somnium Scipionis*. See also 'The Parliament of Birds', ll.29ff.

310 Robinson suggests that 'Tunis' was picked for the rhyme, but there might be a reference to the fall of Carthage to the Romans in 146 BC, when the city's wealth constituted a great prize.

328–31 Priam was King of Troy, and Hector his son was the principal Trojan hero in the war against the Greeks. Achilles was the Greeks' chief hero. Laomedon, father of Priam, built the walls of Troy.

Medea: daughter of King Aeëtes of Colchis and famed for her skill in magic, she helped Jason to win the Golden Fleece but was deserted by him after bearing him two children, whom she later murdered in revenge.

Lavinia: Aeneas's wife in Italy after he deserted Dido.

Paris: his abduction of Helen from Greece was the reason for the war between Greece and Troy.

368 Octavian either the first Roman emperor, or the later Roman emperor who figures in the Charlemagne romances.

402 Flora: Roman goddess of flowers and the spring.

Zephyrus: the west wind.

435 Chaucer wrongly writes 'Argus' for 'Algus', the French name for the mathematician Ibn Musa.

455 John of Gaunt was twenty-nine when Blanche died. Robinson suggests that, owing to a scribal error, 'v' may have been dropped out of 'xxviiii' in the text.

480 Some critics, following Thynne, the 1532 editor of Chaucer's *Works*, think a line such as 'And thus in sorrow left me alone' has dropped out; hence the irregular numbering.

512 Pan: probably introduced here as the god of harmonious nature, to whom unnatural grief would be an affront.

567–71 The *Remedia Amoris* of the Latin poet Ovid (43 BC–18 AD). Orpheus, whose lyre was given him by Apollo, could charm savagery and suffering with his music. In Hades, where he went in search of his wife Eurydice, he lulled the tortures of the damned.

Daedalus: the sculptor and architect who made the wooden cow which enabled Pasiphaë, hiding inside it, to mate with a bull; he built the labyrinth in Crete which housed the resulting progeny, the Minotaur, and made the wings which enabled him to flee the King of Crete's wrath.

Galen: the second-century physician, many of whose medical treatises were extant.

Hippocrates: the most famous doctor of antiquity, by whose name doctors swear when they take the Hippocratic Oath.

589 Sisyphus: better known for his torment in Hades, where he had everlastingly to roll a huge rock up a hill, than for his evil life on earth for which he was so condemned.

663 Attalus III Philometor: King of Pergamum in the second century BC; fabled inventor of chess, but actually a renowned murderer of relations and friends.

667 Pythagoras (*fl.* 530 BC): the polymath from Samos who settled in Croton in southern Italy, and was famed for his mystical religion, philosophy, ethics, mathematics and music. Probably mentioned here because chess may be thought of as a quasi-mathematical activity.

709 Tantalus: often associated with Sisyphus on account of his torment in Hades. But Tantalus is more akin to Prometheus, since his crime, for which he was especially *tantalized*, was giving away secrets told him by Jove.

717 Socrates (469–399 BC): the Athenian philosopher and teacher, cited here for his power to endure hardship with equanimity.

726–33 The stories of Medea, Phyllis and Dido, treated by Chaucer with emphasis on their good faith when deserted by bad men, are respectively the sixth, eighth and third stories in 'The Legend of Good Women'.

736 Echo: a mountain nymph who occupied Juno by talking so that Jupiter could be free to make love to the other nymphs. Juno found out, and punished her by investing her with the qualities of echo, that is, to speak only after others. She fell in love with Narcissus and, when her love was not returned, in her grief she dwindled to a mere voice.

738 Samson (= Hebr. solar): for the whole story, see Judges 14–16.

759–804 A conventional process in the courtly adept's upbringing is described here.

805ff. Again, a conventional account of the loved one: the dancing troop of ladies, the ravishment of music, the idealized physical and moral description.

824 The 'starry seven' may be the Great Bear or the Pleiades.

948 Blanche: the first mention of the name of John of Gaunt's first wife.

983 The self-begetting phoenix, first mentioned by Herodotus, was legendary for the beauty of its red and golden feathers, for its solitariness and for its immortality. It was unique because single.

987 Esther: by her beauty and courtesy charmed King Xerxes of Persia (Ahasuerus) into virtuous action (see the Book of Esther).

1019–33 It was a standard practice in courtly love for the lady to send her suitor off on a dangerous quest without promising love. The Gobi Desert ('dry sea' in Chaucer) and the Black Lake were on the route to China—that is, just about as far away as can be imagined.

1057 Alcibiades: the rich and powerful friend of Socrates, and a paragon of masculine beauty.

1070 Dares the Phrygian (i.e. Trojan): a priest mentioned in the

Iliad; but his supposed account of the Trojan War seems to be late Latin, possibly of the twelfth century. Polyxena was one of Priam's daughters, and the story that Achilles went unarmed into Troy to woo her, and was there killed by Paris, is one of several versions of Achilles' death.

1072 Minerva (*Gr.* Athena): goddess of power and wisdom.

1081 Penelope: the exemplar of wifely fidelity, who remained true to her husband Odysseus during his twenty years' absence, first at the siege of Troy and afterwards on his wanderings.

1084 Titus Livius: the Roman historian Livy (59 BC–17 AD) who is cited in *Le Roman de la Rose* as the author of the story of Lucrece, the historical Lucretia (see the fifth story in 'The Legend of Good Women').

1114 A strange development. The Dreamer, as a means of prompting further easing confession, pretends to assume that, since Blanche deserted the sorrowing knight, the latter will not be guilty if he subsequently loves another.

1118–23 A short catalogue of evil counsellors. Achitophel mis-advised Absalom in his wars against his father David (Judges 2.17); Antenor first advised his fellow Trojans to return Helen to Greece, and then helped Odysseus to capture Troy's Palladium (statue of Pallas Athena), thus virtually ensuring the fall of Troy; and Ganelon, jealous of Roland's warrior prowess, planned with the Moorish king the ambush at Roncesvalles in which Roland and Oliver were killed in 778.

1162 Jubal (erroneously Tubal in Chaucer): in the mythopoeic opening chapters of Genesis (4.21), 'the father of all such as handle the harp and organ'.

1169 'Aurora, a Latin metrical version of parts of the Bible, with allegorical interpretation by Petrus de Riga, Canon of Rheims, in the twelfth century' (Robinson, p.886).

1247 Cassandra: prophetess and daughter to Priam, who after the fall of Troy was taken by Agamemnon as his slave to Mycenae, where Clytemnestra murdered them both. Her lament for Troy was much expanded by the medieval Troy romancers.

1318 It is generally thought that these indications refer to the castle of John of Gaunt at Richmond, Yorkshire. 'Long Castle' may refer to the House of Lancaster, John of Gaunt's family, and possibly the *white* walls refer obliquely to Blanche.

THE HOUSE OF FAME

Title: In the Retraction at the end of *The Canterbury Tales*, Chaucer refers to this work as 'The Book ... of Fame', which is a better title as the house of Fame is only one of three buildings in which the main action of the poem takes place.

63 The insistence on 10 December has tempted commentators to seek a topical reason; but I like David M. Bevington's observation (in 'The Obtuse Narrator in Chaucer's *House of Fame*', *Speculum*, April 1961) that in the calendar then prevailing, 10 December was the winter solstice. The longest night of the year might yield the longest (and best?) dream. The date falls in Sagittarius, the presiding sign of the House of Dreams.

65 The classification of dreams here is hard to make sense of; possibly Chaucer meant it to be so, in harmony with his consistent characterization of the Poet-Dreamer as an earnest novice.

66 Each of the three books of 'The House of Fame' has an Invocation; the other two are modelled on Dante, but the origin of the first one is less clear, though Robinson sees it as deriving from Froissart's *Trésor Amoureux*.

71 Lethe: the underworld river, of which souls of the dead drank and thus forgot all they had said and done in the upper world.

73 Cimmerians: according to Homer, dwellers farthest west in the ocean (i.e. nearest the sunset, which was thought to be the abode of the dead).

103 The story of Croesus and his dream is the last of the monk's examples of the fates of famous men in *The Canterbury Tales*.

116 Holy Leonard: near to Chaucer's house in Aldgate there were three churches dedicated to St Leonard, the patron saint of prisoners. The present reference seems to contain a private joke. Chaucer's Prioress evidently came from the Benedictine nunnery of St Leonard's at Stratford-atte-Bowe, and Chaucer knew people who had visited it, and almost certainly would have been there himself. The distance of two miles is about right.

130 Venus (*Gr.* Aphrodite): goddess of love, whose functions

physical and spiritual were heavily exploited by medieval courtly poets.

138 Cupid (Gr. Eros): son and companion of Venus; usually a wanton young god who inflames sensual passion and promotes not only that, but also discords in love. His mythical predecessor, the older god Eros, represented the uniting power of love which brought order and harmony out of chaos.

139 Vulcan (Gr. Hephaestus): the lame god of fire, consort of Venus and haunter of volcanic islands.

148 Lavinium: Latin city founded by Aeneas and named after his Italian wife, Lavinia.

152 Sinon: the Greek who feigned a defection to the Trojans so that he could persuade them to allow the Wooden Horse into Troy. It was full of Greeks, and when Sinon let them out, the fall of Troy was assured.

158–61 Ilium: strictly speaking, the citadel of Troy. Pyrrhus (or Neoptolemus) was one of the leaders inside the Wooden Horse, and killed the King of Troy and his son at the altar of Jove.

168 Anchises: in youth beautiful enough to attract Venus, on whom he begot Aeneas.

175–8 Iulus: the same as Ascanius. In the *Aeneid*, Creusa became separated from Aeneas while escaping from Troy.

203 Aeolus: in Homer, Aeolus was not god of the winds but an island ruler to whom Jove gave power over them. A later tradition made him a god who kept the winds enclosed in a mountain.

226 Achates: a faithful friend of Aeneas.

236 Carthage: centre of Phoenician influence in the western Mediterranean, a sister city of Tyre in the east, and Rome's deadly rival. Tradition places the founding of Carthage about a hundred years earlier than that of Rome, in about 850 BC. Just before it fell to Rome in 146 BC, its population was about 700,000.

378 The story of Dido and Aeneas, which figures more fully as the third tale in 'The Legend of Good Women', is in Book IV of the *Aeneid*.

379 'The Epistle' is the seventh of the *Epistolae Heroidum* (letters of heroines) of Ovid.

388 The story of Phyllis and Demophon is the eighth in 'The Legend of Good Women'.

398 The catalogue of unfaithful lovers, drawn mainly from Ovid, continues:

Achilles gave Briseis away to Agamemnon after being persuaded by Athena.

Paris rejected his wife Oenone when he carried off Helen.

For the tale of Jason and his desertion of Hypsipyle and Medea, see the fourth story in 'The Legend of Good Women'.

When Hercules captured Iole and took her for his lover, Deianira his wife soaked his shirt in the blood of Nessus the centaur, whom Hercules had killed for making advances to Deianira. The dying centaur had told her that his blood would preserve Hercules' love for Deianira, but it burned him to death. Iole married Hercules' son.

For an account of Theseus and his desertion of Ariadne, see the sixth story in 'The Legend of Good Women'.

429 'The book' is Virgil's *Aeneid*, the story of which is now very briefly summarized to line 465.

441 Sybils: women with second sight.

443 Palinurus: the steersman of Aeneas's ship (l.435 above), who went to sleep at the tiller, fell overboard, and was murdered when he was washed ashore.

444 Deiphobus: another of Priam's sons. He was killed and mutilated by the Greeks during the sack of Troy, and in that condition was found by Aeneas in the underworld.

449 Claudian: a Latin writer of the late fourth century AD, often cited by Chaucer.

457 Turnus: a southern Italian king, killed by Aeneas during the latter's conquests leading to the founding of Rome. Latinus was allied to Aeneas, to whom he wedded his daughter Lavinia, though the latter had been promised to Turnus.

514–16 Of these Dreamers, Scipio (see 'The Parliament of Birds', pp.129ff.), Isaiah (whose *visions*, rather than dreams, are mentioned in Chapters 1 and 6), Nebuchadnezzar (Daniel 1–4) and Pharaoh (Genesis 41) are well known, but there is apparently no certainty about Turnus and Helcanor.

518 Cypris: one of the names of Venus, who was born in Cyprus.

521–2 Parnassus: mountain home of the Muses. Helicon, though called a fountain sacred to the Muses, was in fact a mountain too.

588–9 Elijah 'went up by a whirlwind into heaven' (2 Kings 2.11), and Enoch 'walked with God: and he was not; for God took him' (Genesis 5.24). Romulus, the mythical founder of

Rome, after reigning for thirty-seven years, was carried up
to heaven in a fiery chariot by Mars during an eclipse of the
sun. Ganymede, the beautiful boy whose name gives us the
word *catamite*, was taken up to heaven by Jove, who came in
the form of an eagle.

712 The favourite author was, of course, Ovid, whose description
of the House of Fame is in Book XII of the *Metamorphoses*.

730 The idea that everything has a natural habitat is a medieval
commonplace.

763 This theory of sound is again common, and Chaucer (*v.* Robin-
son, p.765, note) probably found it in Boethius' *De Musica*.

915 According to medieval legend, Alexander was 'carried in a car
in the air by four gigantic griffins' (Robinson, p.765, note).

920 Icarus: son of Daedalus (see note to 'The Book of the Duchess',
l.569). He flew too near the sun and the wax binding of his
wings melted, so that he was drowned in what became
the Icarian Sea. The legendary event is the subject of a
famous painting by Brueghel, and a famous poem by Auden,
'Musée des Beaux Arts'.

932 The 'eyryssh bestes' of Chaucer's original were probably the
signs of the Zodiac, though Robinson surmises that they
were 'the daemons of the air'.

939 It seems that the Milky Way was in each country given the
name of a prominent long road.

942 Phaeton: a favourite classical subject for medieval moralizing.
The son of Helios, the sun, he persuaded his father to let him
drive the chariot of the sun across the heavens. But the
horses proved too strong for him, and when the sun left its
usual path, Jove killed Phaeton with a flash of lightning for
his presumption.

985 Marcian: a fifth-century writer on astronomy.

986 Anticlaudian: a philosophical poem by the twelfth-century
writer Alanus de Insulis.

1004–7 Constellations. Arion (Arion's harp) is Lyra; Castor and
Pollux are Gemini; Atlas's seven daughters are the Pleiades.

1021 Saint Julian: the patron saint of hospitality.

1035 Chaucer *would* make his Dreamer swear by St Peter when
thinking of sea crashing against *rocks* ('petra' being the Latin
word for stone or rock).

1066 Saint Clare: a thirteenth-century abbess and disciple of St
Francis; now patron saint of good weather and of television.
Nuns of her order are called 'Poor Clares'.

Notes to 'The House of Fame'

1076 J. A. W. Bennett (*Chaucer's Book of Fame*, p.98) notes that the Eagle's answer to the poet's question (l.1060) whether humans are making the noise embodies the 'truth that as a man speaketh, so is he'; and further, that the phenomenon described 'symbolizes an aspect of the imaginative process as operating in the poet whose influence has pervaded this second book; for the shapes embodying human speech correspond to those shades in Dante that embody the mental state of men in life'.

1183 Saint Giles: a sixth- or seventh-century saint celebrated in *The Golden Legend* as the patron saint of cripples. Churches dedicated to him were usually on city outskirts, cripples and beggars not being allowed through city gates. Cripplegate disappeared from the map of the City of London in 1981, owing to the Barbican development.

1201 Orpheus: see note to 'The Book of the Duchess', l.568.

1205-7 Some interestingly chosen musicians of fame:

Arion: a citharist of the seventh century BC. He won a music prize in Sicily, and when returning by ship to Corinth he threw himself overboard to avoid being murdered by the sailors for his wealth. Music-loving dolphins took him safely ashore.

Chiron had been taught music by Apollo; he became tutor to Achilles and many other Greek heroes.

Glasgerion: a king's son who was a harpist, and hero of the ballad 'Glasgerion'.

1227-9 This list is evidently of arrogant and bad musicians. Nothing is known of Atiteris and Pseustis, and the story of Marsyas is told in the verse.

1243-6 Now for trumpeters: Misenus for Hector and Aeneas, and Joab for King David (see 2 Samuel 2.18 and 20).

Thiodamus was a Theban augur, whose invocations would be followed by trumpet-calls.

1271ff. Magicians now, female first:

Medea, when forsaken by Jason, murdered her children by him, poisoned his new wife and flew to Athens in a chariot pulled by winged dragons.

Circe: Medea's aunt, who turned men into pigs, often after they had been her lovers.

Calypso: like Circe, detained Odysseus amorously on his homeward journey after the fall of Troy. She could bestow immortality.

241

Hermes Belinous: disciple of Hermes Trismegistus, the Greek god related to the Egyptian god Thoth who was the source of knowledge and thought.

Simon Magus trafficked in black magic during the time of Nero (first century AD). Trafficking in sacred things, including religious offices, is still called simony.

Elymas (in Chaucer, Limote): the sorcerer mentioned in Acts 13, is thought by Robinson to be the person referred to here.

Colle: probably an English magician who practised in Orleans (Robinson, p.894). Chaucer calls him a *tregetour*, a word derived from the French and apparently applied particularly to magicians specializing in illusions, like the man described in 'The Franklin's Tale' (ll. 1140–51 in Robinson).

1327 Surcoat: an outer garment, usually sleeveless, which was often worn over armour.

1352 The Lapidary: an eleventh-century treatise on precious stones.

1383 For 'the feathered creatures four', see Revelation 4.6–8.

1400 Calliope: the Muse of Epic Poetry. The Nine Muses were sisters.

1414 For Hercules' death, see note to l.398.

1432 Robinson suggests (p.895) that since Saturn was the senior planet, the term was applied to Jewish religion as the source of other religions.

1433 Josephus: a first-century Jew who became Romanized and was the author of two books on Jewish history.

1460–70 The first-century poet Statius was not a native of Toulouse. He wrote the *Thebaid* and the *Achilleid*, and in the former tells of an incident in which three Greeks were killed by tigers.

Dictys is supposed to have written a diary of the Trojan War. He and Dares Phrygius (see 'The Book of the Duchess', note to l.1070) provide many of the Troy legends of which medieval poets made use.

Lollius: identity uncertain.

Guido: the author of a medieval Latin history of Troy, based on a French *roman*.

Geoffrey of Monmouth, in his *History of the Kings of Britain*, collected history and myth about early Britain and made Britons descendants of Aeneas, thus qualifying him, for Chaucer's present purpose, as one who 'penned the fame of Troy'.

1499 Lucan: a first-century Latin poet whose chief work was the

Pharsalia, an account of the struggle between Caesar and Pompey.

1509 Claudian: see note to l.449.

1511 Pluto: king of the underworld; Proserpine was his queen.

1547 Fame and Fortune make good sisters, but it is not known whether Chaucer had any authority for making them so.

1796 Isolde: daughter of the King of Ireland, whose lifelong love for Tristan (I use the name forms made familiar by Wagner), in spite of her marriage with King Mark, made her an ideal of love-worthiness and beauty for medieval romancers.

1840 'stripe' and 'bell', i.e. dressed like a Fool.

1869 No identity is proposed for the new character, whose sole function seems to be to ask the questions the answers to which define the poet's attitude to his discoveries thus far.

1920 In his creation of the house of rumour, Chaucer goes far beyond his source, the description in Book VIII of Ovid's *Metamorphoses* of the curious building Daedalus built for Minos to house the Minotaur.

1928 No reason for the choice of the Oise, except its rhyme sound, has been adduced.

2158 A tantalizing non-ending, since the poem cries out for rounding off at this point. Noble patrons' names, as well as neglect by a copying scribe, have been tentatively suggested, as has the God of Love. The ending Caxton supplied is as follows:

> And wyth the noyse of them wo
> I sodeynly awoke anon tho   [at once then]
> And remembryed what I had seen
> And how hye and ferre I had been
> In my ghoost and had grete wonder
> Of that the god of thonder
> Had lete me knowen and began to wryte
> Lyke as ye have herd me endyte
> Wherfor to studye and rede alway
> I purpos to doo day by day
> Thus in dremyng and in game
> Endeth thys lytyl book of Fame

(Quoted by Robinson, p.1018)

THE PARLIAMENT OF BIRDS

1   Chaucer's adaptation of the Hippocratic tag, *Ars longa, vita brevis est.*

31   *Scipio's Dream* (*Somnium Scipionis*): part of Book VI of Cicero's *De Re Publica*, a work on good government and the duty of the citizen, now lost. The section on Scipio was preserved by the fourth-century writer Macrobius, who added a lengthy commentary.

36ff.   Both Scipio the Younger (l.36) and Scipio Africanus (l.40) met Masinissa, the long-lived King of Numidia, who at first sided with Carthage; when Scipio Africanus drove the Carthaginians out of Spain in 206 BC, Masinissa became an ally of Rome. The meeting with Scipio the Younger would have taken place during the Third Punic War (149–146 BC), at the end of which Carthage was destroyed by the Romans.

63   The reference is to the so-called Music of the Spheres, the heavenly sound which Pythagoras thought the planets made in their motion.

117   Some critics have looked for astronomical dating of the poem from this apparent reference to the position of the morning star. But I prefer the view of others that the phrase is to be compared with Hamlet's 'I am but mad north-north-west', and see the statement as yet another of Chaucer's rueful admissions that he was an unsuccessful lover (at least, he offers that persona of himself).

127   A strong echo of Dante's inscription over the gates of hell (*Inferno*, III, 1ff.), but Chaucer's double development indicates two possible outcomes of Love.

170   Like other guides (such as Virgil, who took Dante to Paradise, and the puppy in 'The Book of the Duchess'), Scipio now disappears.

212   Cupid: see note to 'The House of Fame', l.138. Here his malignant function in producing unhappy love is made clear.

218–29   Allegorical personages from *Le Roman de la Rose*, whose detailed functions are not called into action in this poem, need not detain us. For brief information, see any literary encyclopedia or companion; for a stimulating and entertaining discussion of the work, see C. S. Lewis's *The Allegory of Love*, pp.115–56. Chaucer is in fact following a passage in Boccaccio's *Teseide* here.

243 A significant departure from the source Chaucer is notionally
following, which shows the fineness of the poem's design.
Patience's face is pale, and she is placed on a hill of sand. As
J. A. W. Bennett says (in *The Parlement of Foules*, p.91), these
facts 'presage disappointment and sterility rather than glad
submission or eventual fruition'. The end of the poem shows
impatience procuring fruition for all but the four eagles, who
must patiently bear the consequence of Nature's ruling.

254 Priapus: the Roman god of fertility, inflamed with desire,
approached the sleeping nymph Lotis, who was awakened
by the braying of a donkey, and so was able to escape.
Chaucer emphasizes the god's state by making him hold a
sceptre, which is not mentioned in his immediate source,
Boccaccio. The god's phallus, rather than his head, might
well be garlanded, especially by female worshippers. But no
doubt Chaucer has done enough to establish physical urge
'in pride of place' in the Temple of Venus.

275–6 Bacchus (*Gr.* Dionysus): god of wine and ecstasy. Ceres (*Gr.*
Demeter): goddess of the earth and all its fruits. Both deities
of plenty and fulfilment appropriately placed near Venus.

281 Diana (*Gr.* Artemis): twin sister of Apollo, with cognate female
powers of wisdom and healing. But she figures in late
tradition as the chaste goddess of animals and hunting, as
here.

286–92 Here is Chaucer's catalogue of those whose love brought
disaster, drawn from Boccaccio and Dante (who, of course,
drew on classical literature):

Callisto was loved by Jove, and accordingly killed by Diana
on the instruction of the jealous Juno.

Atalanta profaned a grove sacred to Jove by making love
there, for which she and her husband were turned into lions.

Semiramis: the legendary co-founder of Nineveh who so
charmed King Ninus, her husband, that he allowed her to
reign for five days. She used the time to kill him off, and then
embarked on a reign of marvellous achievement, ending her
life forty-two years later by flying to heaven in the form of a
dove. She was noted for her voluptuousness.

Candace: a queen of Tarsus who, according to a medieval
story, enchanted Alexander the Great to indolence.

Byblis, unable to stifle her love for her brother, who fled in
horror, was turned into a fountain by sympathetic nymphs.

Scylla: the daughter of King Nisus of Megara (Alcathoe in the story of Ariadne in 'The Legend of Good Women') who, out of love for Minos, betrayed her besieged city and her father and was drowned by Minos for her trouble.

The 'mother of Romulus' was Rhea Silvia, a vestal virgin who was raped by Mars and so became the mother of the founder of Rome.

Troilus, a younger son of Priam, loved Cressida. Their story is told in Chaucer's poem and in Shakespeare's play.

309 Saint Valentine's Day: St Valentine was clubbed to death in Rome on 14 February 269, for being a Christian. The Valentine's Day customs – of sending love presents and declarations anonymously, of the right of women to proposition men – were apparently already old in Chaucer's time. Many poems celebrate the festival, and all indicate it as a courtly, not a folk, occasion.

316 Alan: Alanus de Insulis, a twelfth-century Latin poet, on whose work *De Planctu Naturae* Chaucer draws for the ensuing passage.

331 An ancient tradition, going back at least to Isaiah and mentioned in the medieval bestiaries, credits the eagle with the power to gaze at the sun. The eagle as king of the birds was a symbol of Christ; most commentators think Chaucer had in mind various social classes or groups when he distinguished between categories of birds. The traditional bird-lore upon which Chaucer draws in ll.330–364 is still mostly current; even Robinson does not comment on all. The most complete list of suggestions that I have found is in D. S. Brewer's edition of the poem (pp.115–18).

373 I retain the medieval word 'formel' rather than its (barely adequate) modern equivalent, 'female'. It applied only to eagles and hawks; a female hawk was better than a male for hawking and, surmises the *Shorter Oxford Dictionary*, was accordingly called 'formal', that is, 'proper'.

380 '...hot and cold, and moist and dry': a conventional reference to the four temperaments or humours, based on combinations of the four supposed elements in medieval physiology.

393 Tercel: the male of any kind of hawk.

583 The turtle-dove: traditionally the advocate of fidelity in love, and clearly a different bird from the 'meek-eyed dove' of l.341 which was especially associated with Venus.

THE LEGEND OF GOOD WOMEN

Title: The work is referred to in the Man of Law's introduction to his tale as 'the Seintes Legende of Cupid' ('The Legendary of Cupid's Saints'), which describes the poem more appropriately than the title in common use, and incidentally makes a usefully ironic connection between Christianity and the religion of Love.

16 Saint Bernard: Abbot of Clairvaux in the twelfth century, famed for his wisdom. The proverbial saying that even he didn't know everything seems to have been common.

70–80 The Flower and the Leaf were rival sets of allegorical values which figure in the amusements of contemporary adepts of courtly love. Those who declare themselves for the Flower bloom briefly and beautifully in love, while those who support the Leaf naturally represent more stable and sober virtues. In the allegorical poem of the early fifteenth century called *The Flower and the Leaf*, formerly thought to be by Chaucer, followers of the Flower indulge in delights, while followers of the Leaf are brave and chaste. The latter comfort the former after a storm has drenched them.

111 The attribution of perfume to the scentless daisy was a commonplace of courtly literature.

130 The two lines following l.130 are added from the 'F' text, ll.143–4.

131 Saint Valentine: see note to 'The Parliament of Birds', l.309.

179 Here, and again at ll. 317 and 422, the poet names the queen of the god of love, and yet at l.505, in answer to the god's question, he behaves as if he did not know she was Alcestis until told. Since the 'mistake' is common to both versions of the Prologue, I prefer to think that the character of the poet in the poem must be seen as deferring, very politely and in some trepidation, to the monarch of the occasion. His ensuing compliment evidently goes down very well with Alcestis (l.523).

186 It has been suggested that Chaucer intended there to have been nineteen 'Cupid's saints'.

203–23 The lovers and beauties here invoked include eight of the ten heroines of 'The Legend of Good Women', Medea and Philomela being excluded. Notes on the other characters follow:
Absalom: King David's son, beautiful and golden-haired, but treacherous. For his story, see 2 Samuel, 13–18.

Esther: see note to 'The Book of the Duchess', l.987.

Jonathan: son of King Saul and close friend of David. See 1 Samuel, 18–20.

Penelope: see note to 'The Book of the Duchess', l.1081.

Marcia: wife of the Younger Cato (95–46 BC), who gave her to his friend. On the death of the latter she returned to her former husband.

Helen: a special representative of beauty because she became the ostensible cause of the Trojan War when Paris abducted her from her husband, Menelaus.

Isolde: see note to 'The House of Fame', l.1796.

Alcestis: eponymous heroine of Euripides' play. When Death came for her husband Admetus she offered herself instead. Hercules brought her out of Hades and reunited her with Admetus.

Lavinia: see note to 'The Book of the Duchess', ll.328–31.

Polyxena: see note to 'The Book of the Duchess', l.1070.

Hero: a priestess of Aphrodite and lover of Leander, who nightly swam the Hellespont to visit her. When he was drowned in a storm she threw herself into the sea.

Canacee (the double 'e' aids correct pronunciation and scansion): daughter of Aeolus and mother of several children by Neptune. She was killed by her father because she fell in love with her brother.

256 'Heresy': see Introduction, p.154.

280 Livy: the Roman historian Titus Livius (59 BC–17 AD), probably cited here because he wrote on the story of Lucrece (Lucretia). Valerius: a Roman author?

281 Jerome: St Jerome (c. 347–c. 420), main author of the Vulgate, wrote *Adversus Jovinianum* 'to refute the contention (among others) of a monk called Jovinian that "a virgin is no better as such than a wife in the sight of God"' (Robert P. Miller, ed., *Chaucer Sources and Backgrounds*, p.415; a generous selection from the Jerome work appears in the book).

305 Ovid's *Epistle* is his *Epistolae Heroidum* (*Heroides*), in which there are twenty-one letters, some of which Chaucer used in writing 'The Legend of Good Women'.

307 Vincent of Beauvais: a thirteenth-century Dominican and author of *Speculum Historiale* (The Mirror of History).

354 Lords of Lombardy: no precise reference is traced; possibly the political turbulence of the region had already become proverbial.

365 Aristotle: not mentioned in Chaucer's text, which has 'the philosophre'. But his advice to kings in Book V of the *Nicomachean Ethics* was also cited by Chaucer's fellow-poet Gower, and in any case, Aristotle was *the* philosopher for the Middle Ages.

382 'The compassion of lions, on the contrary, is clear from innumerable examples – for they spare the prostrate; they allow such captives as they come across to go back to their own country: they prey on men rather than women, and they do not kill children except when they are very hungry' (twelfth-century Latin bestiary translated by T. H. White, *The Book of Beasts*, Jonathan Cape, 1954, p.9).

408 Arcite and Palamon and their love for Emily are the subject of the first of *The Canterbury Tales*, 'The Knight's Tale'.

411 Roundel: see 'The Parliament of Birds' (ll.680–92) for an example.
Virelay: a thirteenth-century French dance-song, usually of three stanzas. Each stanza is preceded by the two-line refrain, and then follows the four-line stanza, the last two lines of which use the music of the refrain. Then the second singing of the refrain ends the stanza.

414–18 If this is a true account of Chaucer's subject matter, then his work based on Innocent III's commentary on Boethius and on Origen's homily has not survived. Origen (*c.* 185–*c.* 253), a defender of Christianity and especially the upholder of mystical interpretation of the Bible, was a controversial but important figure in the early Church. When young he made himself a eunuch 'for the kingdom of heaven's sake' (see Matthew 9.12). The Life of Saint Cecilia is presumably 'The Second Nun's Tale'.

464 A standard defence, in all times up to but not including our own, of those accused of writing immoral material is that it is done to warn against evil.

480 Another of Chaucer's frequent protests (or laments?) that he himself is not engaged in the kind of passionate action of which he writes.

500 The turning of Alcestis into a daisy seems to be a Chaucerian invention (Robinson). 'Day's eye' is the correct etymology for 'daisy'.

514 Agathon (*c.* 447–400 BC): a poet and friend of Plato and Euripides. Probably mentioned here because in Plato's *Symposium*, which was known as 'Agathon's Feast', the story of Alcestis is told.

Notes to 'The Legend of Good Women'

519 Cybele (*Gr.* Rhea): earth goddess and mother of both Jove and Neptune.

580 Ptolemy: the thirteenth Egyptian king of that name, whom Cleopatra murdered so that she might reign alone. This is F. N. Robinson's numbering, following 'F' text of the Prologue.

624 Octavian (63 BC–14 AD): Octavius Ceasar the conqueror of Antony and Cleopatra.

634–49 This short passage on the sea-fight off Actium has stimulated a flow of scholarly ink. Every detail of the manner of fighting has been confirmed from contemporary accounts of medieval naval battles, including the practice of spreading some slippery substance on the decks (peas? pease? pitch?) to frustrate foemen's foothold.

696 It was a comparatively common medieval barbarism to put an offender in a snake-pit.

707 Semiramis: see note to 'The Parliament of Birds', l.288.

773 Phoebus: the epithet ('bright' or 'pure') applied to Apollo as the sun god.

774 Aurora (*Gr.* Eos): goddess of the redness of dawn, who announces the coming of the sun and accompanies him throughout the day.

785 Ninus: king, and co-founder, with Semiramis, of Nineveh.

930 Most of the characters mentioned in this second Chaucerian account of the fall of Troy and its consequences figure in 'The House of Fame' (see notes to ll.151–380).

932 Minerva (*Gr.* Athena): goddess of power and wisdom.

942 Ascanius: Aeneas's son.

964 Achates: faithful friend of Aeneas.

1005 Sichaeus: Dido's rich uncle, to whom she had been married. He was killed by Dido's brother Pygmalion, an event which touched off Dido's emigration and the founding of Carthage. Historically, the fall of Troy (*c.* 1184 BC) and the founding of Carthage (*c.* 853 BC) are more than three hundred years apart. It is owing to Virgil and his insertion of the Aeneas episode into the life of Dido that we think of the two events as closely successive.

1245 Iarbas: historically, but not in Virgil, a neighbouring king whose attempt to force Dido into marriage with him caused her to immolate herself.

1297 Mercury: the Roman god of commerce who inherited the characteristics of Hermes, the Greek god used as herald and messenger by the gods.

1383 Possibly, suggests Robinson (p.963), Chaucer echoes a passage in Dante's *Inferno* (XIX.5), where 'the public crying of the misdeeds of condemned criminals' is mentioned. Chaucer clearly gives notice, by blowing a horn, of raising the hue and cry against Jason.

1396 Guido: see 'The House of Fame', note to l.1469.

1425 Colchis: not in fact an island but a region near the Caucasus.

1453 Argus: the grandson of Aeëtes. Jason had rescued him after a shipwreck.

1457 *Argonauticon*: the *Argonautica*, an unfinished heroic poem in eight books by Valerius Flaccus, a first-century poet; known to the Middle Ages chiefly through Dares Phrygius.

1459 Philoctetes: most famous of Greek archers, and friend and armour-bearer to Hercules. Hero of a tragedy by Sophocles.

1466 Hypsipyle: became Queen of Lemnos (the island, incidentally, upon which Philoctetes was marooned by the Greeks besieging Troy, because the stench from his wound lowered their morale) when the women of the island killed all the men except her father, whom she hid, for consorting with Thracian slave women. In Valerius Flaccus the messenger is of course a woman, but Chaucer has a male messenger (l.1486), an error I have corrected.

1679 In this account of Jason and Medea, the latter's sorcery is referred to only obliquely, and her tremendous revenge on Jason – murdering her two children by him, and poisoning his next wife – is not mentioned at all. It figures in Chaucer only as the prophecy of the abandoned Hypsipyle (1574 *ante*).

1682 Tarquin: Sextus Tarquinius, the ravisher of Lucretia, was the son of Tarquinius Superbus (so named on account of his great cruelty). The rape of Lucrece was the last straw for the oppressed Roman people, who banished the entire family, and with it the kingship, in 510 BC.

1689 'Our Legend' is probably *The Golden Legend* (a thirteenth-century collection of largely unhistorical saints' lives). St Augustine comments on the story in *De Civitate Dei* (The City of God) I.19 (Robinson, p.964).

1695 Ardea: the city of the Rutulians.

1710 Collatine lived in Collatia, not Rome. In the full story, the Roman officers first went to Rome, where they found the women of the Tarquin family feasting, and afterwards to Collatia.

1749 A centuries-old commonplace in masculine praise of women.

Notes to 'The Legend of Good Women'

1862 Brutus: Lucius Brutus, the tribune who assumed leadership of the Roman people rebelling against the Tarquins.

1870 Lucrece's Day was 24 February – the date, as it happens, on which first I drafted this note.

1882 The Syrophoenician Woman (Matthew 15.28).

1886 Minos, the King of Crete, was, like his brother Rhadamanthus, the son of Jove and Europa; both after death became judges in the underworld.

1896 Androgeus was not killed out of envy of his prowess at philosophy, but because he beat his fellow-contestants in the games of the Panathenaea.

1902 Megara: a city twenty-six miles from Athens. Its citadel, Alcathoë (l.1922), was named after its founder Alcathous).

1908 For the daughter of Nisus, Scylla, see note to l.292 of 'The Parliament of Birds'. In the myth on which Chaucer draws, she killed her father by plucking from his beard the purple hair on which his life depended. So the city fell; but Minos, horrified by her undaughterly action, drowned her.

1928 The 'monstrous wicked beast' was the Minotaur, offspring of Pasiphae, Minos's queen, by a bull.

1944 Aegeus: King of Athens and father of Theseus. The latter sailed to Crete with black sails. On his triumphant return he forgot to hoist white sails, the agreed signal of his success, and Aegeus, thinking he was dead, threw himself into the sea (hence the *Aegean* Sea).

2155 The island of Aegina is near Athens, in the Saronic Gulf.

2163 To maroon Ariadne on Naxos, Theseus would have had to sail many miles east and south before turning back to Athens. See any map of the eastern Mediterranean.

2223 Taurus: Bacchus took pity on Ariadne, made love to her, and threw her up to heaven as a star in the constellation Hercules.

2237 Primum Mobile: in Chaucer 'the first heaven', i.e. the outermost in the Ptolemaic system.

2247 Pandion: King of Athens.

2249 Juno (*Gr.* Hera): senior goddess in the classical pantheon, protectress of women and especially of marriage.

2250 Hymen: originally a marriage song, but later personalized into a handsome youthful god bearing a marriage torch.

2252 The Furies: goddesses of Vengeance who hunted down criminals. Only in later poetry (e.g. that of Ovid) are they limited to three, and named.

2253 Owl: in Golding's translation of the *Metamorphoses* (VI. 552–3) we have:

> And on the house did rucke [i.e. huddle]
> A cursed Owle the messenger of yll successe and lucke.

2274 Philomela (= lover of song): poetic name for the nightingale (see Introduction, p. 158).

2357 An interesting detail of medieval ladies' education. Presumably, writing was the work of employed clerics, while weaving was an appropriate activity for gentlewomen.

2367 Another messenger who was traditionally – and more appropriately – female, Chaucer makes male.

2384 The subsequent revenge of the sisters, in killing Tereus's child and serving him cooked to his father, is not germane to Chaucer's tale!

2398 Demophon: son of Theseus and Phaedra.

2421 Neptune (*Gr.* Poseidon): the god hostile to the Greeks, whose ships returning to Greece from Troy he pursued with storms.

2422 Thetis was a sea-goddess and mother to Achilles. Triton was a half-human, half-fish son of Neptune. Sometimes Tritons are mentioned in the plural. No good explanation of 'Chorus' here exists.

2425 Lycurgus: according to Boccaccio, the King of Thrace.

2438 Rhodope: a mountainous region of Thrace.

2570 Danaus and Aegyptus were twins. Danaus had fifty daughters, and Aegyptus fifty sons who proposed to their cousins. Danaus's daughters were instructed by their father, who feared his nephews, to kill their husbands in the bridal bed. All did except Hypermnestra, whose husband Lynceus later killed Danaus. In Chaucer, Aegyptus (after whom Egypt is named) was father to the daughters.

2630 The Fatal Sisters: the three Parcae, or Fates – 'Clotho (who held the distaff), Lachesis (who spun the thread of life), and Atropos (who cut it off when life was ended)' (Rev. Cobham Brewer, *Dictionary of Phrase and Fable*).

2723 No satisfactory explanation exists for the failure to round off this tale.

SELECT BIBLIOGRAPHY

Since Chaucer is a major poet whose work has attracted a huge
mass of critical writing, the problem of providing a useful and
manageable bibliography for a book of this kind is not a slight
one. In offering the following suggestions I have in mind
students from sixth-form to degree level, as well as general
readers who wish to push their interest in Chaucer and these
four poems further than the limited introductory material and
notes to this edition allow them to go. I am not thinking of either
budding or mature medievalists, who in any case have no need
of a book of translations of Chaucer. My list of recommended
books, which has been pared down from a longer one, is there-
fore of books recently written and, I hope, easily available. I list
no articles, though some of the most valuable essays appear in
books listed below. The Humanities Index and other relevant
subject indexes in good libraries will assist readers who wish to
go even further.

1. A good, because straightforward, beginning to a study of
early Chaucer would be to read:

> S. S. Hussey, *Chaucer: An Introduction* (Methuen, 1972),
> Chapters 1 ('Poet and Public') and 2 ('Dreams and Their
> Dreamers').

Two books which vividly re-create the world of Chaucer, as
far as historical records and the evidence of contemporary
literature allow, are:

> John Gardner, *The Life and Times of Chaucer* (Granada, 1977)
> Derek Brewer, *Chaucer and His World* (Eyre Methuen,
> 1978).

Three books on important influences on Chaucer, the first two of which examine how he transformed what he borrowed from others and with what effects, now follow. The Windeatt book is especially complete and useful in relation to the four Love Visions.

Charles Muscatine, *Chaucer and the French Tradition* (University of California Press, 1957)
John M. Fyler, *Chaucer and Ovid* (Yale University Press, 1979)
B. A. Windeatt, *Chaucer's Dream Poetry: Sources and Analogues* (Boydell Press, 1982)
Robert P. Millar, *Chaucer Sources and Backgrounds* (Oxford University Press, New York, 1977) contains translations of many key passages from the Latin, French and Italian authors on which Chaucer drew, as well as some English ones, but the book also deals with the whole range of the poet's work.

2. Now to the core works of criticism, only five of which I list below:

J. A. W. Bennett, *Chaucer's Book of Fame: An Exposition of 'The House of Fame'* (Oxford University Press, 1968)
J. A. W. Bennett, *The Parlement of Foules: An Interpretation* (Oxford University Press, 1957)
Robert Worth Frank, Jr, *Chaucer and 'The Legend of Good Women'* (Harvard University Press, 1972)
John Norton Smith, *Geoffrey Chaucer* (Routledge & Kegan Paul, 1974)
A. C. Spearing, *Medieval Dream-Poetry* (Cambridge University Press, 1976).

Two collections of critical essays should now be mentioned:

Derek Brewer (ed.), *Geoffrey Chaucer* ('Writers and their Background' series, Bell, 1974) is a compendium of essays by distinguished scholars, and is especially recommended.
Edward Wagenknecht (ed.), *Chaucer and Modern Essays in*

Criticism (Oxford University Press, 1959) contains the following four useful essays:

> Bertrand Bronson, 'The Book of the Duchess Re-opened';
> Paul G. Ruggiers, 'The Unity of Chaucer's House of Fame';
> Charles O. Macdonald, 'An Interpretation of Chaucer's Parliament of Fowls';
> D. D. Griffith, 'An Interpretation of Chaucer's Legend of Good Women'.

A further useful critical work on early Chaucer is:

> P. M. Kean, *Love Vision and Debate* (Volume 1 of *Chaucer and the Making of English Poetry*, Routledge & Kegan Paul, 1972).

3. Recommended Further Reading:

> C. S. Lewis, *The Allegory of Love* (Oxford University Press, 1936), especially Chapters I to III
> Dorothy Everett, *Essays on Medieval Literature* (Oxford University Press, 1955), Chapters IV, VI and VII
> D. W. Robertson, Jr, *A Preface to Chaucer: Studies in Medieval Perspectives* (Princeton, 1962)
> D. W. Robertson, Jr, *Essays in Medieval Culture* (Princeton, 1980), Parts I and V.

For those interested in 'the colours of rhetoric', that is, the figures of speech and the stylistic devices which Chaucer used so plentifully in these four poems, but discussion of which I have had to omit, an explanatory book is:

> J. W. H. Atkins, *English Literary Criticism: The Medieval Phase* (Cambridge University Press, 1943; Methuen, 1952).

Lastly, there is a collection of views of Chaucer – one would hardly call most of it literary criticism – through the ages down to 1933, linked by an editorial commentary:

> Derek Brewer (ed.), *Chaucer: The Critical Heritage 1385– 1933*, 2 vols (Routledge & Kegan Paul, 1978).

INDEX OF PROPER NAMES

Index

Index

Index

Index

Index

READ MORE IN PENGUIN

In every corner of the world, on every subject under the sun, Penguin represents quality and variety – the very best in publishing today.

For complete information about books available from Penguin – including Puffins, Penguin Classics and Arkana – and how to order them, write to us at the appropriate address below. Please note that for copyright reasons the selection of books varies from country to country.

In the United Kingdom: Please write to *Dept. EP, Penguin Books Ltd, Bath Road, Harmondsworth, West Drayton, Middlesex UB7 0DA*

In the United States: Please write to *Consumer Sales, Penguin USA, P.O. Box 999, Dept. 17109, Bergenfield, New Jersey 07621-0120*. VISA and MasterCard holders call 1-800-253-6476 to order Penguin titles

In Canada: Please write to *Penguin Books Canada Ltd, 10 Alcorn Avenue, Suite 300, Toronto, Ontario M4V 3B2*

In Australia: Please write to *Penguin Books Australia Ltd, P.O. Box 257, Ringwood, Victoria 3134*

In New Zealand: Please write to *Penguin Books (NZ) Ltd, Private Bag 102902, North Shore Mail Centre, Auckland 10*

In India: Please write to *Penguin Books India Pvt Ltd, 706 Eros Apartments, 56 Nehru Place, New Delhi 110 019*

In the Netherlands: Please write to *Penguin Books Netherlands bv, Postbus 3507, NL-1001 AH Amsterdam*

In Germany: Please write to *Penguin Books Deutschland GmbH, Metzlerstrasse 26, 60594 Frankfurt am Main*

In Spain: Please write to *Penguin Books S. A., Bravo Murillo 19, 1º B, 28015 Madrid*

In Italy: Please write to *Penguin Italia s.r.l., Via Felice Casati 20, I–20124 Milano*

In France: Please write to *Penguin France S. A., 17 rue Lejeune, F–31000 Toulouse*

In Japan: Please write to *Penguin Books Japan, Ishikiribashi Building, 2–5–4, Suido, Bunkyo-ku, Tokyo 112*

In South Africa: Please write to *Longman Penguin Southern Africa (Pty) Ltd, Private Bag X08, Bertsham 2013*

PENGUIN AUDIOBOOKS

A Quality of Writing That Speaks for Itself

Penguin Books has always led the field in quality publishing. Now you can listen at leisure to your favourite books, read to you by familiar voices from radio, stage and screen. Penguin Audiobooks are produced to an excellent standard, and abridgements are always faithful to the original texts. From thrillers to classic literature, biography to humour, with a wealth of titles in between, Penguin Audiobooks offer you quality, entertainment and the chance to rediscover the pleasure of listening.

You can order Penguin Audiobooks through Penguin Direct by telephoning (0181) 899 4036. The lines are open 24 hours every day. Ask for Penguin Direct, quoting your credit card details.

A selection of Penguin Audiobooks, published or forthcoming:

Little Women by Louisa May Alcott, read by Kate Harper

Emma by Jane Austen, read by Fiona Shaw

Pride and Prejudice by Jane Austen, read by Geraldine McEwan

Beowulf translated by Michael Alexander, read by David Rintoul

Agnes Grey by Anne Brontë, read by Juliet Stevenson

Jane Eyre by Charlotte Brontë, read by Juliet Stevenson

The Professor by Charlotte Brontë, read by Juliet Stevenson

Wuthering Heights by Emily Brontë, read by Juliet Stevenson

The Woman in White by Wilkie Collins, read by Nigel Anthony and Susan Jameson

Nostromo by Joseph Conrad, read by Michael Pennington

Tales from the Thousand and One Nights, read by Souad Faress and Raad Rawi

Robinson Crusoe by Daniel Defoe, read by Tom Baker

David Copperfield by Charles Dickens, read by Nathaniel Parker

The Pickwick Papers by Charles Dickens, read by Dinsdale Landen

Bleak House by Charles Dickens, read by Beatie Edney and Ronald Pickup

PENGUIN AUDIOBOOKS

The Hound of the Baskervilles by Sir Arthur Conan Doyle, read by Freddie Jones

Middlemarch by George Eliot, read by Harriet Walter

Tom Jones by Henry Fielding, read by Robert Lindsay

The Great Gatsby by F. Scott Fitzgerald, read by Marcus D'Amico

Madame Bovary by Gustave Flaubert, read by Claire Bloom

Mary Barton by Elizabeth Gaskell, read by Clare Higgins

Jude the Obscure by Thomas Hardy, read by Samuel West

Far from the Madding Crowd by Thomas Hardy, read by Julie Christie

The Scarlet Letter by Nathaniel Hawthorne, read by Bob Sessions

Les Misérables by Victor Hugo, read by Nigel Anthony

A Passage to India by E. M. Forster, read by Tim Pigott-Smith

The Iliad by Homer, read by Derek Jacobi

The Dead and Other Stories by James Joyce, read by Gerard McSorley

On the Road by Jack Kerouac, read by David Carradine

Sons and Lovers by D. H. Lawrence, read by Paul Copley

The Prince by Niccolò Machiavelli, read by Fritz Weaver

Animal Farm by George Orwell, read by Timothy West

Rob Roy by Sir Walter Scott, read by Robbie Coltrane

Frankenstein by Mary Shelley, read by Richard Pasco

Of Mice and Men by John Steinbeck, read by Gary Sinise

Kidnapped by Robert Louis Stevenson, read by Robbie Coltrane

Dracula by Bram Stoker, read by Richard E. Grant

Gulliver's Travels by Jonathan Swift, read by Hugh Laurie

Vanity Fair by William Makepeace Thackeray, read by Robert Hardy

Lark Rise to Candleford by Flora Thompson, read by Judi Dench

The Invisible Man by H. G. Wells, read by Paul Shelley

Ethan Frome by Edith Wharton, read by Nathan Osgood

The Picture of Dorian Gray by Oscar Wilde, read by John Moffatt

Orlando by Virginia Woolf, read by Tilda Swinton

READ MORE IN PENGUIN

A CHOICE OF CLASSICS

Francis Bacon	**The Essays**
Aphra Behn	**Love-Letters between a Nobleman and His Sister**
	Oroonoko, The Rover and Other Works
George Berkeley	**Principles of Human Knowledge/Three Dialogues between Hylas and Philonous**
James Boswell	**The Life of Samuel Johnson**
Sir Thomas Browne	**The Major Works**
John Bunyan	**The Pilgrim's Progress**
Edmund Burke	**Reflections on the Revolution in France**
Frances Burney	**Evelina**
Margaret Cavendish	**The Blazing World and Other Writings**
William Cobbett	**Rural Rides**
William Congreve	**Comedies**
Thomas de Quincey	**Confessions of an English Opium Eater**
	Recollections of the Lakes and the Lake Poets
Daniel Defoe	**A Journal of the Plague Year**
	Moll Flanders
	Robinson Crusoe
	Roxana
	A Tour Through the Whole Island of Great Britain
Henry Fielding	**Amelia**
	Jonathan Wild
	Joseph Andrews
	The Journal of a Voyage to Lisbon
	Tom Jones
John Gay	**The Beggar's Opera**
Oliver Goldsmith	**The Vicar of Wakefield**
Lady Gregory	**Selected Writings**

READ MORE IN PENGUIN

A CHOICE OF CLASSICS

William Hazlitt	**Selected Writings**
George Herbert	**The Complete English Poems**
Thomas Hobbes	**Leviathan**
Samuel Johnson/ James Boswell	**A Journey to the Western Islands of Scotland** and **The Journal of a Tour of the Hebrides**
Charles Lamb	**Selected Prose**
George Meredith	**The Egoist**
Thomas Middleton	**Five Plays**
John Milton	**Paradise Lost**
Samuel Richardson	**Clarissa**
	Pamela
Earl of Rochester	**Complete Works**
Richard Brinsley Sheridan	**The School for Scandal and Other Plays**
Sir Philip Sidney	**Selected Poems**
Christopher Smart	**Selected Poems**
Adam Smith	**The Wealth of Nations** (Books I–III)
Tobias Smollett	**The Adventures of Ferdinand Count Fathom**
	Humphrey Clinker
	Roderick Random
Laurence Sterne	**The Life and Opinions of Tristram Shandy**
	A Sentimental Journey Through France and Italy
Jonathan Swift	**Gulliver's Travels**
	Selected Poems
Thomas Traherne	**Selected Poems and Prose**
Henry Vaughan	**Complete Poems**

READ MORE IN PENGUIN

A CHOICE OF CLASSICS

Matthew Arnold	**Selected Prose**
Jane Austen	**Emma**
	Lady Susan/The Watsons/Sanditon
	Mansfield Park
	Northanger Abbey
	Persuasion
	Pride and Prejudice
	Sense and Sensibility
William Barnes	**Selected Poems**
Anne Brontë	**Agnes Grey**
	The Tenant of Wildfell Hall
Charlotte Brontë	**Jane Eyre**
	Shirley
	Villette
Emily Brontë	**Wuthering Heights**
Samuel Butler	**Erewhon**
	The Way of All Flesh
Lord Byron	**Selected Poems**
Thomas Carlyle	**Selected Writings**
Arthur Hugh Clough	**Selected Poems**
Wilkie Collins	**Armadale**
	The Moonstone
	No Name
	The Woman in White
Charles Darwin	**The Origin of Species**
	Voyage of the *Beagle*
Benjamin Disraeli	**Sybil**
George Eliot	**Adam Bede**
	Daniel Deronda
	Felix Holt
	Middlemarch
	The Mill on the Floss
	Romola
	Scenes of Clerical Life
	Silas Marner

READ MORE IN PENGUIN

A CHOICE OF CLASSICS

Charles Dickens	**American Notes for General Circulation**
	Barnaby Rudge
	Bleak House
	The Christmas Books (in two volumes)
	David Copperfield
	Dombey and Son
	Great Expectations
	Hard Times
	Little Dorrit
	Martin Chuzzlewit
	The Mystery of Edwin Drood
	Nicholas Nickleby
	The Old Curiosity Shop
	Oliver Twist
	Our Mutual Friend
	The Pickwick Papers
	Selected Short Fiction
	A Tale of Two Cities
Elizabeth Gaskell	**Cranford/Cousin Phillis**
	The Life of Charlotte Brontë
	Mary Barton
	North and South
	Ruth
	Sylvia's Lovers
	Wives and Daughters
Edward Gibbon	**The Decline and Fall of the Roman Empire** (in three volumes)
George Gissing	**New Grub Street**
	The Odd Women
William Godwin	**Caleb Williams**

READ MORE IN PENGUIN

A CHOICE OF CLASSICS

Thomas Hardy	**Desperate Remedies**
	The Distracted Preacher and Other Tales
	Far from the Madding Crowd
	Jude the Obscure
	The Hand of Ethelberta
	A Laodicean
	The Mayor of Casterbridge
	A Pair of Blue Eyes
	The Return of the Native
	Selected Poems
	Tess of the d'Urbervilles
	The Trumpet-Major
	Two on a Tower
	Under the Greenwood Tree
	The Well-Beloved
	The Woodlanders
Lord Macaulay	**The History of England**
Henry Mayhew	**London Labour and the London Poor**
John Stuart Mill	**The Autobiography**
	On Liberty
William Morris	**News from Nowhere** and **Other Writings**
John Henry Newman	**Apologia Pro Vita Sua**
Robert Owen	**A New View of Society and Other Writings**
Walter Pater	**Marius the Epicurean**
John Ruskin	**Unto This Last and Other Writings**
Walter Scott	**Ivanhoe**
	Heart of Mid-Lothian
	Old Mortality
	Rob Roy
	Waverley

READ MORE IN PENGUIN

A CHOICE OF CLASSICS

Robert Louis Stevenson	**Kidnapped**
	Dr Jekyll and Mr Hyde and Other Stories
	The Master of Ballantrae
	Weir of Hermiston
William Makepeace Thackeray	**The History of Henry Esmond**
	The History of Pendennis
	The Newcomes
	Vanity Fair
Anthony Trollope	**An Autobiography**
	Barchester Towers
	Can You Forgive Her?
	The Duke's Children
	The Eustace Diamonds
	Framley Parsonage
	He Knew He Was Right
	The Last Chronicle of Barset
	Phineas Finn
	The Prime Minister
	Rachel Ray
	The Small House at Allington
	The Warden
	The Way We Live Now
Oscar Wilde	**Complete Short Fiction**
	De Profundis and Other Writings
	The Picture of Dorian Gray
Mary Wollstonecraft	**A Vindication of the Rights of Woman**
	Mary and **Maria** (includes Mary Shelley's **Matilda**)
Dorothy and William Wordsworth	**Home at Grasmere**

READ MORE IN PENGUIN

A CHOICE OF CLASSICS